# POWER THROUGH WITCHCRAFT

## SUN ☉

SELF AUTHORITY — PRIDE —
SELF EXPRESSION — MALES

## MOON ☽

EMOTIONS — FEMALES —
THE SUBCONSCIOUS WOMEN

## NEPTUNE ♆

INSPIRATION — MUSIC — DESTINY —
THE ARTS — SEDUCTION

## JUPITER ♃

PHYSICAL — GOOD TIMES — LEGAL —
POLITICAL — RELIGIOUS — EXTRAVAGANCE

## PLUTO ♇

UNDERWORLD — UNAVOIDABLE DESTINY —
EXCITING MALES

*figure I*

# POWER THROUGH WITCHCRAFT

by

Louise Huebner

**NASH PUBLISHING CORPORATION**
LOS ANGELES, CALIFORNIA
1969

Copyright © 1969 by Nash Publishing Corporation
All Rights Reserved
Library of Congress Catalog Card Number 73-95367
Standard Book Number 8402-1105-8
Printed in The United States of America

SECOND PRINTING

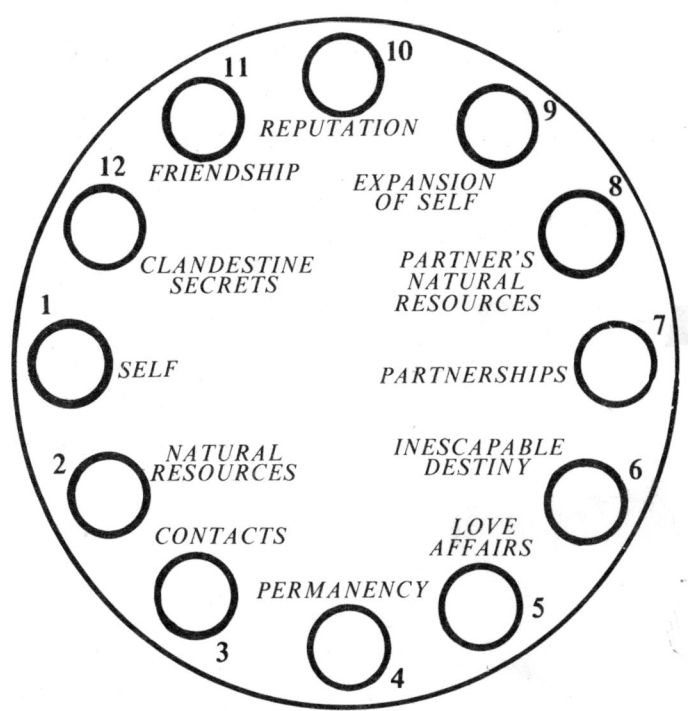

THE CARD SPELL

# POWER
THROUGH
WITCHCRAFT

# 1
# Witchcraft—
# What It's Really Like

*"I'll walk where my own nature would be leading... where the wild wind blows on the mountain-side..."*
Emily Bronte

Witchcraft has survived through the ages with astounding vitality because man's need to coerce destiny and subdue the fear within has never subsided. The art of enchantment attempts to deceive, cajole, and otherwise disturb natural inclinations. Children, politicians, actors and women in love have much in common with sorcerers who, with bits of colors, attitudes and words, weave spells.

Lovers draw or carve a circle or a heart on a tree or wall and put their initials inside, and this is supposed to have the magical effect of uniting them. They are trying to influence their destiny. New brooms are brought into new homes by people with the idea that they won't be bringing the dirt and problems of the old house into a new one. Hanging bright strips of ribbon in your window is supposed to attract friendly spirits into your home, and many people still do this, perhaps without knowing why.

Whether it is considered superstition or lore, witchcraft

comes to us as a gift from the past. But nothing that lives is safe from Time, so that witchcraft, like a story of an ancient battle told and retold through the ages, is tainted by exaggeration and twisted by falsehood as it is handed down through the years.

Originally witches were involved in teaching, guiding and healing—all of the highly respected arts. Their practices were associated with all the vital phases of man: health, wealth and love. In later years, through fear and ignorance, the stamp of evil was placed upon those who possessed these strange powers, so that today witchcraft is either regarded as a complete myth or the misguided efforts of historic villains. There are so many false ideas about witches that little truth remains in the public mind.

Yet there are real witches today. Contrary to folk tales, they don't go riding about by night on brooms. They don't cavort in the nude unless they have something very normal in mind, and they don't cackle over cauldrons of vintage LSD. They DO dabble in spells and chants, burning candles and employing powerful processes, but once the mystery is stripped away, there is nothing much more strange connected with witchcraft than the mysteries of love and religion. In fact, when lovers light candles for dinner, and when churchgoers light candles in prayer, they invoke a force that witches always have known to be beneficial.

What is a witch really like? For one thing, a witch is not an ugly old hag. The very idea is unkind and illogical. If a witch has, as she is said to have, special powers and an ability to disturb natural happenings, then she must be able to project the illusion, if not the truth, of beauty. When one has the power to charm, enchant and fascinate, then it also follows that one has the power to create an aura of pleasing good looks if not something more. If a witch has some secret force that enables her to control and influence others, this ability should certainly lead to an abundant popularity and many successful attractions, rather than to condemnation and repulsion. Who then were the ugly hags called witches? If historical accuracy is lacking as to who

# Witchcraft—What It's Really Like

and what they were, it must follow that there is little truth in how they "seemed" to look.

For a magnificent example of misrepresentation, look at Salem, Massachusetts, in the 1690's: political and religious victims, old tired wives, envied neighbors, folk doctors, hysterical teenagers, menopausal mothers-in-law, the retarded and/or psychotic, unwanted old souls—all were counted as fair and proper witch material. But let's face it: Would a witch with ESP and a strong inclination for survival have ignored the signs of a fast-decaying society and impending personal disaster? Would a witch with energy and power to impose her will have suffered the extremes of personal humiliation? And if, due to some momentary weakness, all else had failed her, couldn't a witch at least have mustered up the strength to manipulate her jurors and thus go free? They were imposters who left Salem rich in history, and the real witches, if there were any, left that city long before the history started. A witch is not an ugly old hag. A witch is a winner. No self-respecting, energetic, good-looking witch would have been caught dead in Salem!

The shape of witchcraft, in history and in legend, has been as varied as the imagination of the witch or personality involved dared. Little in common can be seen between Snow White's beautiful but wicked stepmother with her "Mirror, mirror, on the wall . . . ." and Joan of Arc with her dedication to a cause, unrelenting drive, thirst for adventure and celestial voices. And certainly these two women would never have felt a rapport with mythology's Medea, the sorceress who, when scorned by Jason, gifted his new and very much younger love with a gown of magical cloth that burned as fire. However little there may be to bind these women in a community of interests, it is not too difficult to categorize them by virtue of the *"esprit de corps"* that motivates any enchantress: Those who wish to alter circumstances must be intense, emotional, self-motivated and capable of obsession.

Although popular knowledge of witches comes mostly from fairy tales and legends, not to mention superstition, let us set one thing straight: Witches are human, very human, and sometimes a little superhuman. They are physical animals who may have a special mental quirk; supernormal, perhaps, but not supernatural. As to the belief that witches live many lives, it is doubtful.

I am a witch and the only life other than this one that I believe possible would be some extension of self. If it is impossible to explain this thing called self, then it may be possible to entertain the idea that all humans are tuned into a vast, ubiquitous source of energy that enables each individual to think or be. If that were so, then maybe when I am no longer around to tune into that particular force of energy, someone else will, and then the thoughts will exist again, but not necessarily me. If I have lived before, I certainly am not aware of it. And, I don't think I will come back knowing I'm me; in fact I don't think I will come back at all. If I do, I shall be the first one to pass out from shock.

As to whether witches are good or evil, that depends upon your point of view about what's good and what's evil. From the average man's interpretation of evil and good, witches seem to be evil. Organized religions have branded witchcraft as evil, but they did this because they considered witchcraft a form of competition and naturally reasoned that anyone against them would have to be on the side of the devil. There is no such thing as good and evil witches on the basis of one of them deriving their powers from the devil. The power witches tap is an energy inside themselves. It should be considered wasteful, stupid, and therefore bad not to use the energy within one's self to gain one's desires, to fulfill one's self.

Witches *are* selfish, but is that evil? Being self-interested, a witch has to be personally motivated to do anything, anything at all, even to get up in the morning. Witches do not go anywhere they don't want to go or do anything they don't want to do. This kind of an approach to living would naturally enrage churchmen who demand strict obedience to their rigid laws and condemn the nonconformers as satanic or evil. Actually, there were witches before Christianity came along, and although there

# Witchcraft—What It's Really Like

have always been evil gods in religions in all parts of the world, Satan exists only in limited areas. So who would witches be in cahoots with in, say, China? Selfish, yes; in league with the devil, no.

Many similarities can be seen between the attitudes of witches and those people who are successful doing anything. There's a big difference between having things turn out well and having things turn out badly. If you want them to turn out well, you're bound to have something in common with someone else who has things turn out well, even if you're doing it one way and he is doing it another.

Witchcraft is simply a form of self-promotion. People have always secretly agreed to the existence of witchcraft, and it may be that they have become more open about it (not I—I always have been open about it!) Everyone I talk to, even if they do not want the public to know that they believe in this sort of thing, will confide their belief to me. I've never felt the least bit odd or self-conscious about doing what I do or being what I am, because everyone always admits that they believe in what I do. They may not tell each other, but they tell me—doctors, lawyers, and other professional men who don't want their clients to know that they believe in magic. Most doctors readily believe in witchcraft, but they believe anybody can develop it. Many agree that it exists. Of course, I admit that to a certain extent, anyone can do anything. I believe, however, that there is a big difference between the chants or spells cast by a nonwitch and those done by a lifelong witch, if only from the standpoint of experience and power of controlled emotions.

Witches are sharp people. If they're not above average in intelligence, they're above average in cleverness, and they don't get into unhappy situations; they are productive types, and they're always successful in what they attempt.

Most of the so-called witches in Salem were victims of circumstances. The cases you read in reference books point out that witches usually were somebody's unwanted mother-in-law or an old grandmother whose family couldn't support her anymore and so would accuse her of witchcraft. But the greatest percentage were religious–political victims, because at that time the church was in a frenzy, and the religious leaders felt the more witches they got rid of, the better became the church's reputation. So they looked all over hell-and-gone to find witches. It was very simple. Mental defectives were easy to eliminate. People of power were a bit more difficult, but it didn't prevent them from eradicating a few mayors and governors, too.

Mass hysteria is commonplace in any era. Just look at what Hitler did by turning "Jew" into an evil word. Nor was 20th-century America immune. Joseph McCarthy had the same effect with the word "Communist." Remember what happened to the Indians? So many dollars per scalp. Those bounty hunters were direct descendants of the witch hunters of the 1600's who made a pretty penny by turning in their neighborhood nuisances under the handy label of "witch."

Even so, fewer witches were put to death in Salem than in England or France. The fad didn't last as long here. The European witch hunters received a yearly stipend to go from city to city, and when they arrived in a new city, they would set up a little office and then find local assistants who were also paid for finding witches. Soon the whole town would be involved in a nightmarish hysteria. Chemists and doctors were prime targets, understandably. Medicine was so primitive, mistakes were bound to occur; it was easier to attribute a death to witchcraft than to a dirty scalpel or the wrong medication.

Personally, I don't believe any of those people were witches. Most of the cases have been investigated and proved to be something other than supernatural. In those days, if they suspected someone of being a witch and then found a wart on her, that was all the proof needed to make her eligible for a hideous death.

And all the time the characteristics of the real witch were overlooked. The magnetism and forceful personality that characterized the authentic witch were never seen in an evil light. It was only the poor helpless woman or the politically inept man who were swept up and tortured until they confessed to practicing witchcraft. The accused, in turn, would helpfully accuse almost anyone they could think of, thus causing large numbers of innocent people to suffer a painful death.

Sex was a distinct liability in those days. The servant-girl mistress of a well-placed man could easily find herself hunted down by a "virtuous" mob if she proved troublesome to her benefactor. It didn't do to look too appetizing, either. A sexy-looking girl was thought to have charms, (which indeed she did) but these were invariably evil charms, and she could not be allowed to display them. On the other hand, things haven't changed too much on that score! An exotic, sexy-looking lady is frequently looked upon with suspicion and hostility in certain of our communities, even today.

When accused witches were brought to trial, the questions they were asked were of the "When did you stop beating your wife?" genre. Women were asked to admit they were having sexual relations with the devil, and under torture they admitted it. I find it very difficult to accept the idea of the devil romping around and mating with all these warty women. If he did exist, it seems to me he could have done a lot better choosing ladies more like Sophia Loren or Brigitte Bardot, perhaps.

At one time chemists were considered magicians. Albertus Magnus (1193–1290), considered a wizard in his day, was responsible for the discovery of caustic potash, cinnabar, and ceruse. He was a leader in witchcraft. You may remember his name from the film *Rosemary's Baby*. He was a chemist who was preoccupied with turning other metals into gold by (transmutation) alchemy. In the course of his experiments he discovered things that were to be of far more value to succeeding generations than a pot of gold.

Potassium bicarbonate was discovered by another alchemist of that era. Sulfuric ether and hydrochloric acid were other compounds the alchemists discovered as they practiced their kind of witchcraft. The existence of gas, sodium sulfate, phosphorus and tin oxide were other discoveries made during that period. In the course of their experiments, these men chanted, lit candles and did all sorts of weird things and, as a result, became the forerunners of the abracadabra type magician.

Even today you see things happening that resemble the witch hunts of old. Once, a mother-in-law wrote to me, convinced her daughter-in-law was a witch. The girl had pointed teeth, and she did have a few quirks in her behavior, but the mother-in-law must have spied on every move the poor girl made, even in the bathroom. The woman had kept some kind of record to prove that every time the girl did a certain thing, some relative in the family would die within a few days. Sometimes, reading mail like that makes you fear that the whole world has gone mad! Here was this woman taking out her hatred of her daughter-in-law, and connecting all sorts of unrelated events to prove the girl was a witch. If that had happened 200 years ago in Salem, they would have burned the girl.

I had a lovely woman acquaintance, a divorcée with two children, who worked very hard. Her capable, fifteen-year-old son would watch his ten-year-old sister after school until his mother got home from work. One day she came home and they were gone. She found a notice from the police stating that they had taken the children away on the grounds that she was an unfit mother. The neighbors had turned her in! She didn't even know her neighbors except to say "Hello," but evidently they were very interested in her. And that happened in the 1960's. It's easy enough to see how things were twisted in the unenlightened 17th century.

We Americans were originally Puritans and any unconventional behavior was taboo. An immoral affair may have seemed "witchy" merely because it was considered a terrible sin. We should remember that we were a bit "different" to begin with, as we left one society, the old world, in order to find a better one, the new world. Obviously, people don't leave the society in which they are born unless there is some incompatibility in the first place.

Put enough of these "different" people together, and something is bound to happen. High-class, well-fed, well-adjusted people are not going to leave their communities. Rarely will somebody make such a drastic move, uprooting himself from his native soil, for some kind of ideology. Not if he is happy. The people who came here and set up the colonies and their rules were of a lower class, and they were hungry. Many had left home due to emotional problems. Looking back on their stage of history, one can understand the people and events.

There *were,* however, educated people who practiced witchcraft. It is known that Jackson and Benjamin Franklin dabbled in it. They surmised that environment could be controlled through emotional self-control. Franklin investigated this area quite extensively. Abraham Lincoln had some strange ideas; he had several psychic experiences that are recorded in the history books. This phenomenon is not unusual among powerful men in any society. Rasputin in Czar Nicholas' court attempted to exert control through sorcery. MacKenzie, the Canadian prime minister, openly delved into the supernatural. Many professional men and women and political leaders practice forms of witchcraft, although what they do seems to be much more fun than what took place a few hundred years ago. There is, for example, a political organization that meets regularly for the purpose of projecting its desires onto society. Call it witchcraft or not, they perform special rituals to trigger their collective subconscious. They attempt to influence and control by sheer force of desire.

Witches have always been linked to strange happenings—good, bad and always mysterious. And when astounding things happen, it doesn't take much imagination to see how witchcraft could have started and spread as it did. Everybody's imagination was captured by the idea of this power, which is actually only a way to reinforce the mind's potential.

As noted, the earliest witches were alchemists whose prime concern was discovering a chemical way to create gold. And there were women who taught young girls how to capture their true loves by digging certain roots under certain lunar phases. However, these women weren't really witches; they were superstitious peasants, thoroughly steeped in herbal lore, who lived throughout most of the European countries.

Herbs were used extensively in ancient Rome, as well. They were not only employed for refreshment, but also burned as offerings to the gods. Frequently, inhalation of certain fumes would cause odd reactions, which led to the belief that various herbs had magical properties. As one conclusion generally leads to another, certain effects were often attributed to various substances, thus somewhat removing the substances from their originally intended purposes. Rosemary, for example, was thought to improve the memory. From that premise, it developed into a love potion, as it was presumed that the herb would prevent a young man from forgetting the lady who administered to him. This is just one example of the way in which spells and potions usually ended up with a kicky romatic flavor.

Of course, many herbs are still very much in use. A well-known cough medicine uses an herb that has been prized for centuries. Digitalis, once a witch's love potion because of its obvious effect on the heart, is still a standard medicine for cardiac patients. Then there are the *real* love potions, those substances that cause sexual stimulation, such as Spanish fly and the other cantharides. And, of course, there are those that have the opposite effect, like saltpeter, which is extensively used in the military and in prisons to keep the men cooled off. The pharmacopeia is loaded with products whose bases are roots and herbs that have always been known to witches.

People used to believe that witches caused sterility. Well, I've got news for you: They still do. Last year I was contacted by a family who believed that the husband had been hexed and as a result was sterile! In another case a doctor from UCLA sent two women to me after they had been checked out at the campus, and he asked me to look into the possibility that they had been hexed. He was an accredited doctor—a psychologist—who wears the cloak of respectability to the extent of having offices on the campus of a highly respected university, and then he sends patients to a witch to be dehexed. So are you going to call a witch crazy? People constantly write to me in the belief they have been hexed; they've consulted with medical or other authorities who *agreed* and suggested the patient call a witch to see if the spell could be broken.

Of course, being hexed does happen. A hex occurs when

you allow some other people to exert control over you, when you surrender your own control to whatever the force may be, and let it take over. To combat a hex, you must simply take control of yourself. An occasional thought might slip into your mind—it happens to everyone—that you're no good or that you're failing. But immediately when this hits you, you must counteract it and supersell yourself in the other direction. Thoughts are very powerful. Thoughts are all we are, all we're made up of.

Most people have experienced the power of psychic vibration, although many don't realize what it is. It's that feeling of instant recognition that flows between two people, like electricity. Sometimes it's mistaken for "love at first sight," many times as a strong sexual attraction. In actuality, it's the psychic force emanating from the individual, not the individual himself, which causes the attraction. Two people may be operating on the same wave length, the same level of psychic energy; when that happens, they zing into each other like two strangers in a foreign land, drawn to each other by a common bond of nationality. It's not necessarily love, or even sex. It's psychic attraction and should be recognized as such.

This is not to say that witchcraft and love are incompatible. Even our language reflects the similarities in the two. Such words as charm, enchant, fascinate, and casting a spell are common to both worlds. When you fall in love, you feel as though you are under a magic spell. The fact that love is an unseen force does not make it any less real; a psychic involvement has occurred.

The same sort of psychic exchange happens when I cast a horoscope. During the time I work on an individual chart, I feel drawn to the subject, almost as though I were in love with him. I know it isn't love, but simply a concentration of psychic energy at work. But the force *feels* the same. With this knowledge, it seems strange to me that people can accept the energy force of love, yet refuse to acknowledge that other forms of psychic exchange can take place, such as mental telepathy.

Almost everyone has, at one time or another, experienced

forms of psychic energy. We all know the common occurrence of suddenly thinking of someone we haven't seen in a long time, only to receive a phone call from him shortly thereafter. Or having letters cross in the mail, indicating that you and a parted friend had simultaneous thoughts of each other. It may be as simple a thing as wishing you had some ice cream, only to have your husband stop and buy some on his way home, with no word from you. Or it could be an incident as disturbing as having foreknowledge of a death or accident to a loved one, sometimes at the very moment the tragedy is occurring.

Incidents like these are the result of free, high-level energy flowing between individuals. Is it not then possible to conceive of controlling and directing this type of energy for your own use or to help others? This is what a witch does.

Many nonwitches have and use this power. The friend who visits a dying hosptial patient, and by the very force of his emotional energy revives the ill person, is an example. More common is the appearance of a strong personality into a confused, panicky situation, like an office crisis. The individual who exudes composure and control can use his strength to pull the rest of the people into a calm, unified, problem-solving group. Nothing in the situation has changed, nothing has been said, but the atmosphere has been altered. It is simply a matter of one person being able to harness the wild energy around him and controlling it. Anyone who learns to do this cannot help but improve his life circumstances.

And that's the witch's bag in a nutshell. She knows how to put the power of her secret mind to work, how to harness the wild energy around her. But not all witches do their thing the same way.

Some witches always begin with a romantic interlude. The charged atmosphere between a male and a female cannot be duplicated, and it does generate high-intensity energy. That's why the stories of sexual orgies involved with witchcraft got started. But that certainly is not what witchcraft is all about, even if some groups use it as an excuse for wild sexual excesses, which sometimes include sadomasochistic practices. It's too bad that these groups get so much publicity, because it leads the general public to believe that's what witchcraft is all about. Nothing could be further from the truth.

Don't get me wrong: If a person gains energy by taking his clothes off, I'm all for it. There are witches who cast spells in the nude, and are thereby utilizing a way to become dynamic. Some witches use drugs to heat themselves up for spellcasting, although I don't believe in that. I would never take chances with anything that might harm me physically, and rather than experiment with drugs, I experiment with life.

One of the reasons witchcraft and sex are closely allied is the psychic feeling that can easily be confused with a sexual feeling. Psychics have sensations all over their bodies, as do all sensating creatures. We feel *all over* a sensation similar to that of sexual arousal when we "tune in." We experience a sexual, sensual, physical and emotional sensation that is all-pervading, but it's not in the pubic region. The confusion probably arises because the only time most people have experienced this kind of sensation is in a sex situation, so naturally it is associated with that. However, if you experience the feeling because it's a nice day, you can't go to bed with the universe. Some people can't understand that there is something else going on besides the need to go to bed. This joyful, exhilarating sensation can be experienced just through being alive.

Witches are far from extinct: They are not even rare. And people who are psychic have always been around. They may be very telepathic, and they may be picking up somebody else's energy without being a practicing witch. Strange things happen to them, seemingly unexplainable, and people marvel at it all. Criswell, the world famous predictor, told me that when he was a youngster he would stand on top of a hill and feel godlike. I've had the same sensation, ever since I can remember. It's a feeling of being all-powerful, knowing there wasn't anything I couldn't do or be if I wanted to. Maybe that's just being healthy, but I'm sure everyone doesn't feel that way.

I've known about my power since I was a schoolgirl. I knew that I could make my teachers do what I wanted just by concentrating. The more successful I was, the more powerful I felt. I would do little experiments, like deciding what a person would say, then making them say it. It may be that I was simply manipulating them, setting them up to react in a certain way, but the method isn't important. It's the result that counts.

When I was a child, my mother and my grandmother did all sorts of psychic, witchy things, so they naturally recognized that I was a bit different from the rest of my cousins. My sister doesn't do this. She is a medium: She receives, which makes her very important to anyone who is a witch. I have been psychic since childhood. People used to visit us, and I could tell them things about their lives that I could not possibly have known if I hadn't been psychic. Frequently, people would react in a nervous way, and of course, any child enjoys causing a sensation in adults, so I kept it up. I soon learned to differentiate between true psychic vibrations and imagination. When I'm receiving a psychic impression, my whole body is involved. I *know* I'm right, and if I'm not sure, then I'm not receiving in a psychic way. There's never any doubt in my mind.

All of my family were involved in astrology, which has nothing to do with witchcraft. My grandmother was especially creative. She wrote songs, both words and music, and she sculptured and did many other things that might be considered a bit above normal. She was very far out for her generation; consequently she was a loner, although she managed to have eight kids.

She could break a glass by using her mental strength and nothing else. She had tremendous strength and energy that could be felt. She'd place a glass in the center of the table and I could feel a concentration of energy coming from her and know she was going to break that glass. Without touching it, just sitting there, and turning on this power, the glass would shatter.

I don't know what that psychic force is. She could make something at a distance rattle, and I imagine she'd be very good material for some psychic investigators. She'd CALL bugs into the house. An insect would fly through the window when she said it would, and then she'd put her hand out, and it would come to her. She could get a praying mantis to come in just by saying she would. The insect would come in through the window, come to the table and sit on her hand. She spoke to it in Yugoslavian or English or Italian, or she'd sing and hum; she'd say, "C'mon, C'mon, I love you," and she'd charm it in.

I lived with my grandmother most of my life from the time I was six until I was 20. She taught me astrology, palmistry and how to read cards and tea leaves. She told me stories about the Pagan gods and the symbolism involved and how to apply it to everyday living. She taught me to be a witch. It was a crazy way to grow up, but it was fun.

I always knew about fortune telling. My grandmother and I established such a good rapport, that we could each project into the other one's house and know what was needed—as though we had shown up to ask. Things like that make you know very early in life that there is no limit to the mind's power.

If witchcraft is a mental power, why do witches usually use props? I use candles, bells and other things to get into the mood, because I was raised to believe they were necessary. But I believe a very strong person can do without the candles and other objects. My grandmother feels that the flame of a candle can change the atmosphere and can create vibrations; that may be true, although I'm not sure. I know I'm becoming more and more able to cast spells without props, but I'd rather use props because I am comfortable with the old methods.

There's nothing wrong with using candles and other props to condition and key up your senses. For ages, religions have employed candles, bells and incense to affect the concentration of their congregations. Lighting candles, as is done in church, can be done at home for the same purpose. It's not such a hokey thing that it should occur only in the dominion of witches. Many clever people in all professions are aware of the power of objects.

A bell is supposed to attract the spirits, and it may, but I believe spirits are energy from within yourself or from within other people. What does ringing the bell in church mean? It may be that the bell sets into motion some sort of electrical vibrations in the atmosphere that eventually lead to something. I use bells in much the same way as Pavlov did. I am conditioned to hear the bell, and I say, "Okay, my subconscious has now taken over."

Anything that will stimulate your senses can help. The bell is for the ear, the candle for the eyes, incense for the nose; they get all the senses working. Some people prefer to cast spells nude; others like to wear clothing with a pleasing texture. Some people cast spells right before they make love. Everybody does it differently. The whole point is to become stimulated enough.

All witches are not the same. I have a good witch friend who never uses candles. She draws designs to release her powers, although drawing does nothing for me. It's simply a question of conditioning. What works for one witch may not work for another. The only thing that my friend and I have in common, as she's more of a housewife-type witch than I am, is the need to absorb everything around us in order to possess it. That goes for people as well as opportunities and situations. We both are able to get out of ourselves and use our minds independently of our bodies.

I have another friend, a man who is considered a wizard. He's very psychic and can move objects by mental power alone. He uses no props at all, not even a candle. He doesn't need to, as he is a very strong type and extremely self-confident.

Every once in a while I find a psychic who likes to hinge what he does on an exotic past. I'm sure you've met people who say that in another life they lived in Turkey or Arabia or some other exotic place. If they get their kicks that way, and if that gives them energy and power, then I'm all for it. If the designs my friend uses trigger something for her, I think she should use them all of the time. She has a happy, productive life, and I think that's the goal we all are seeking.

It's all right to be a little bit odd today. Before, if you were a little odd or different, you were considered completely psycho; now, however, so much is being accepted that it's very difficult to find the borderline. It seems sometimes that there is no norm. Most of the people who are interested in witchcraft want to know about spells, and particularly how to increase their sexual vitality, to capture or keep somebody . . . it's never to get rid of somebody or decrease something, it seems.

Almost anybody can benefit from the powers of witchcraft. It's a lot more than just a positive way of thinking. It taps a source of power far greater than the conscious mind.

The power of positive thinking is one thing, but with witchcraft you use something other than your conscious mind. I believe positive thinking works to a certain degree, but how do you keep your thinking positive? No matter how strong you are, your subconscious is going to trip you up. You can't sustain a positive thought without thinking something negative is going to happen. What you must do is perform a certain ritual that reinforces the positive thought when it starts to slip. That's witchcraft. That's when you start using objects to do the work of your mind.

An object that has no connection with your purpose, but in which you believe, can be used. For example, if you believe in a certain cup, and if you put it beside the phone with the thought that your lover will call because of it, that's more than positive thinking. When your lover does telephone, that's witchcraft.

# 2
# The Tools of Witchcraft

> *"O'r folded bloom, on swirls*
> *of musk, the beetle booms adown*
> *the glooms and bumps along the dusk ..."*
> James Whitcomb Riley

How can you use the powers of witchcraft for yourself? Does it mean a dangerous involvement with covens, warlocks, psychics, familiars, fortune tellers and the spirit world? Most of these questions stem from popular misconceptions of witchcraft. Real witchcraft can be as sensible as a blue-chip stock investment, and often a lot less complicated. Witches aren't creatures of a dark, shadowy world. A modern witch is more likely to be a swinger in mini or mink.

To practice witchcraft, you don't have to join your local sex orgy club. There are witches who argue that total abstinence from sex is better for casting spells. Others who practice witchcraft believe an orgy is necessary. They argue that right before the sex act there is special energy in the atomosphere. That may be true, but how long can you sustain that high state of energy? Not long. You can concentrate on witchcraft, or painting, medicine or bookkeeping better when you're not distracted by sexual

# The Tools of Witchcraft

tension. The only connection between witchcraft and sex is that both thrive on high-voltage energy. The mystics in India attempt to sustain that particular state over a long period of time for various aesthetic reasons, but even then it reaches a peak without the sex act and dissipates itself naturally. By freeing yourself, you control yourself. You can only control what is out and around, not what is hidden. Freedom goes along with control. People who are not free are unable to control themselves. They are slaves to the inner mind. That may sound like a contradiction, but I have never believed that suppression indicates control. You don't control a wild horse by merely keeping him chained; you control him by teaching him how to use his freedom. Freeing your suppressed, untapped inner power is what witchcraft is all about. What most people fail to understand is that witchcraft is the conditioning and strengthening of your subconcious so that this brain potential can be realized.

The first thing you must do to succeed in witchcraft is to learn to love yourself. You must become selfish to *thenth* degree. People really are selfish, but they are taught to disguise it. Self-interest is a strong trait in anyone who gets ahead. A painter, for example, could not succeed in his work if he stopped painting everytime a friend dropped by or his wife nagged about being lonesome. He has to be selfish with his time or else he cannot paint. There's no time to waste worrying about somebody else's interpretations.

If you want something, you first have to recognize what it is that you want. You have to become completely involved with what you want, or else you're not going to get it. You've got to be obsessed by it and work at it all of the time. You can't be witchy part of the time and hope to achieve full success.

Are there dangers involved in practicing witchcraft if you're a novice? A novice is one who's not a real witch, but one who's using the powers. The only danger is that you'll probably improve your character and increase your emotional strength. I don't think there's any "danger" attached to that idea. There *is* a real danger, however, if you believe that witchcraft means consulting evil forces and having conversations with the devil.

But if you understand witchcraft as a way of disciplining your mental and emotional attitudes, then it can only lead to successful conclusions.

There are some clubs practicing storybook witchcraft; their real bag seems to be perversion. The members are just a group of frustrated people looking for kicks. Has anyone ever come across any of these orgy fans who ever expressed any intelligent attitude about their witchcraft? All this mystery and hiding is simply because there is nothing there. When there's really something going on, you should be able to express it and bring it out in the open.

Then there's the old lady from England who gives lectures at $2.50 per admission and pulls in crowds of 40, 50 and 60 people at a time. She promptly tells the audience that she's psychic, but then she doesn't give any psychic readings. She tells the people she's a witch, but doesn't explain what witchcraft does. If you sign up for a $75 course, she will tell you a bit more about how great she is, but she never will tell you what to do. I think there's nothing much that she knows except how to take advantage of people's misinformation.

There is a big gap between popular conceptions of witchcraft and what it really is. Take the very successful book and film *Rosemary's Baby,* which was a lot of fun, but was based on a false premise. In the story, the devil was behind it all. Rosemary, the main character, was fed a mixture that created a strange effect on her mind (which can happen in witchcraft, of course). The story conveys other truths about witchcraft, but the mixture of truth and error, fact and fantasy, confuses people. Objects play an important part in the practice of witchcraft in *Rosemary's Baby.* For instance, I make lucky rocks for people who are my friends, and these objects can give the receiver the emotion of confidence, because, naturally, when you receive a gift from someone who has put something of himself into it, it has an effect on you. However, unlike the witches in *Rosemary's Baby,* real witches aren't anticipating the birth of an Anti-Christ. You must believe in Christ before you seek his opposite,

# The Tools of Witchcraft

and most witches have no leanings toward any orthodox religion.

Despite the growing popularity of witchcraft, there has been little accurate information available describing it as it really is today. The mass conception of witchcraft has been exploited and fed by those profit-seekers who have captured the peoples' imagination, using the half-truths everyone is familiar with. *Rosemary's Baby* is a good example of what witchcraft is supposed to be, but at no point does the movie pull the true picture into view. The mental aspects weren't touched upon at all, and that is the heart of it: to bring an individual under control through your own emotional energies.

Other aspects of witchcraft you must learn about are the psychics, real and phony, the familiars, and the spirits that witches supposedly rub shoulders with regularly. An 18-year-old black cat named Othello is my familiar. A familiar is usually an animal that a witch uses to get energy. I used to have a beautiful female German Shepherd and would receive energy from petting her, because she was so full of life. You're bound to feel turned-on when you're near someone who vibrates with energy. But I can't go for people using a toad as a familiar, because how can you get turned on with a toad? It just doesn't have the same warm, vibrant personality as a dog or cat.

Many people claim that dogs and cats can see the spirit world. They *can* feel and react readily to energy, even your primitive, subconscious force. Witches are supposedly able to take an animal shape, or send an animal on a mission, but that isn't true. Witches assume no form other than their own natural human one.

As far as ghosts or images are concerned, I believe that you can project your personality with enough force so that someone will accept this projection of your personality as you. And it is you, it is the essence of you, minus the physical body.

Are you psychic? If you are, you know it: You're already doing psychic things. There are many schools that attempt to increase a person's psychic awareness, which reminds me a little of dancing schools. That is, you might be able to take a person with an awkward walk, give him dancing lessons to enable him to walk more gracefully, but he'll never be able to rip around the stage in a ballet. <u>Anything can be improved with training, but whether or not you're going to practice witchcraft, you can't be psychic unless you're born that way.</u>

Unlike some people, I never claim to be tapping any supernatural power, or trying to save the world. The pseudopsychics have a gift of sensitivity, but nothing more. Any psychic could pretend to give inside information on the stock market or medicine, but what competent psychic would sell these services, unless he has specialized training as well as sensitivity? That's why I don't like being grouped with the community of psychics. The true psychic isn't about to play the five-dollar-a-session game. Some genuine psychics are so afraid of being lumped with that group, they never mention their powers. A friend of mine is a doctor, a good one, and he is also a psychic. He uses his power in the field of medicine, but only discreetly. Many politicians are psychics, as are many actors and actresses. Most of them aren't aware of their power, but their success is due to the "magical" mass rapport they can instantly establish.

More and more scientific people are coming to believe in a kind of witchcraft. We know animals are aware of certain things instinctively; they are born, generation after generation, with the ability to understand a particular situation that they have not learned from their own experience; there's a kind of instinctive, collective mind between all animals. Researchers have discovered that information lived through the experiences of one rat may be physically induced in an alternate generation by genetic transplants. If this is possible, then the same thing could be possible with humans and would account for many of the situations in which we seem to know the same thing at the same time—or feel it. We've all heard stories about a man inventing some strange new thing, and when he goes to apply for a patent, he discovers somebody else has just been at the patent office with the same fantastic invention. It has happened time and again in medicine, and scientists argue that, naturally, at the conclusion of years of experimentation with processes, a discovery is inevitable. But actually, couldn't it also be true that the thought is there at that time, and many people are tuned-in to it? If that's the case, it could mean that there exists some extension of the conscious mind. And if there is a connection like this, then how could it be unless there were a connection between all our minds? A universal mind.

Perhaps witches are more able to tap this basic power, this universal subconscious, than are ordinary people. This also might explain why there's such an emotional drain on witches, who become horribly depleted at times. I get charged up again, usually by going on radio, as the object of concentration of thousands of people. If I go on one good show, this live audience contact can keep me keyed up for a month, until I begin to feel drained again and need a new transfusion. When I've got thousands and thousands of people tuned in, all concentrating on me, it does something to me, charges my batteries. Energy attracts me. I enjoy being around people who are successful. Mental energy in the raw state can be a tremendous vital source. I don't mean people who have made a fortune, necessarily, but people who are in the process of becoming what they want to be, so that they are active, have a goal in mind and are getting there. When I'm near this kind of person, I get very charged up, and it gives me a lift that lasts much longer than just the instant it takes to communicate with the person. There is energy around people, and I like to be near energy. I'm addicted to it, not just attracted.

There is an ancient belief that there is power in words; this belief is based on the concept that words are symbols of your ideas and thus have a magical quality. We use words to place what is happening in our minds with another person's mind. Some of the older religions still believe that the symbolism of letters is powerful, too. During World War II the Jews in Syria had every reason to believe they were about to be invaded by the Germans. They called up their Cabalists (a body of religious scholars) who spent an evening in meditation. The Cabalists discovered they could manipulate the letters in "Syria" and by reversing them, spell "Russia". After chanting this reversal over and over, they appeared in the plaza and told the assembled crowd to have no fear, the Germans were going to invade Russia, not Syria. The Germans did indeed turn to Russia, but whether or not the Cabala caused this is debatable.

The witches' coven still does exist, even though witchcraft is primarily concerned with the control of your own individual emotions so you can change your own and others' destiny. Witches do at times group together to strengthen their projections. But these gatherings do not have to involve a lot of drinking, steaming cauldrons, stripping and sex. Generally, those of us who are really involved with witchcraft are independent people who do not care about meeting with other witches, except in connection with using each other's energy. All witches need outside help sometimes and will arrange for a group of friends who practice the same type of witchcraft to put all their energy into a single thought at a given time.

Sometimes we get cases in which somebody is cheating—using YOUR energy in a way that was not agreed upon. We try to make it fair. You don't split up the energy so that it is going in all different directions; you take turns. For instance, there were times when we were all concentrating on a particular thing we wanted to happen for me; then I got the feeling that a certain witch in Studio City was not using her power to cast a spell for me, but rather, was working for something to come back *to her*. Witches do tend to cheat, so you always have to be on the watch. Usually we are not physically together; it's just a mental thing. We are together only in that we synchronize a thought to the same moment. An interesting fact is that you can tell who isn't with it, and you can even tell if someone is late, unsynchronized.

That's the closest I ever get involved with a real witches' circle. When we are together physically, everyone is so distracted with the ordinary, everyday things in their minds that the kind of concentration required for a spell is just better done in solitude and at a distance. We work together best if we just state the facts and synchronize. One witch I know takes pep pills around the clock. Because she is quite familiar with the feelings and the high that are produced by pep pills, I call her when I'm going on a radio show and ask her to transfer her sensation of being high to me. By synchronizing we are able to give me the same lift that she gets from the pills.

Sometimes we witches join forces when we want money to come in. People, however, limit themselves without thinking. When you say you want to win money at the races, you have to be able to control the horses, the jockeys, the trainers, the whole thing—and witchcraft isn't a dead-aim shot. So never put a frame around what you want: Play it very loose. When we decide we want money, we never say: "I want money to come in through my husband's job." No, that's too narrow, too limited, and probably not enough anyway.

None of the witches I know are poor, but most are very extravagant. All of us would probably be much better off financially, if we weren't so wild and impractical when it comes to money matters. People often say, "You should be extremely well-off because you do magic." Yes, a witch can be rich, and many are, if that is the way they are concentrating.

The coven in our area is just a loosely associated group. Judging from the mail I receive, I'd say there is at least one person in every community who practices witchcraft. People in every walk of life are witches and wizards. There is a difference, by the way, between wizards and warlocks. A warlock is generally an effeminate male who has a great interest in witchcraft. He never has much success with his spells, which usually backfire or turn out in a way quite different from what he intended. Warlocks lack control of their subconscious. A wizard is the actual male counterpart of a witch. He does have the power of control and knows how to handle it. There is one warlock who calls me all the time, haunts me, is always telling me the results of his experiments with witchcraft and is always coming up with some manifestation of a spirit, which I think is a manifestation of his own goofiness.

Just as you'll find witches everywhere, you'll also have no difficulty finding various types of witchcraft. In Haiti, for instance, the Haitians practice the kind of witchcraft that involves sticking pins into little dolls. These people continually practice voodoo, and the interesting thing is that it works—whether or not you believe in it, or even whether or not you know it's going on. You don't have to be in the know: You can be completely innocent of it, and it still works. It's an example of one subconscious reaching out to another. If your conscious mind *is* aware of what's taking place, then it's certainly incidental.

Caribbean voodoo traffics in fright. It's famous for its use of animal intestines to make special little pouches, or to burn in the same way that we use parchment paper in spells. The whole philosophy is one of death, blood and guts. But witchdoctors do use candles and herbs, too.

Southern European witches used to use locks of hair, nail clippings and occasionally blood from the object of the spell. They believed it was the object itself that had a magical effect. I believe the mental power exerted against the individual cast a conscious spell into his subconscious. Objects are generally used for the confidence they give the person using them. There have been cases in Haiti, for example, where a person was hexed and actually weakened and died as a result. This happens because the person who casts the spell has the power to project destructive thought into the victim's subconscious, through the force created by hatred. And although props are generally used, they aren't indispensable. They have no intrinsic magic, but they can reinforce your faith in yourself.

In selecting the tools of witchcraft, the tasteful, modern-day witch tends to steer way from the gory old items of grandmother's day and backward nations. Candles, bells, flowers, lotions and potions are so much nicer to work with.

Many people carry lucky coins, put horseshoes over their doors or place a rabbit's foot in their pocket. Governor Ronald Reagan wore the same tie throughout his entire campaign because he felt it was lucky for him. I'm not saying he practices witchcraft, but he practices one facet of it: superstitious belief. The first year I was on television, I wore the same green dress on every program. After I built up a little more confidence, I got rid of the dress, but I kept the same earrings all through the next year. For two years I wore the same earrings. I rationalized that I did this because they looked good on me, but I could have found another pair that looked as good at the time. I think that people do this all the time and accept it very casually. Many actors do. They have lucky numbers; they will not associate this with being witchy, just being human. And maybe that's what it is, a human trait.

When Jack Lemmon is about to shoot a take on the film stage, he shuts his eyes and repeats, "Magic time, magic time, magic time." Why does he do that? I'm sure he'd be just as effective without it, but he believes this gives him a boost. Bette Davis had a little gold beetle that she carried with her for luck. Carole Lombard had a little, smooth, white stone that Clark Gable had given her, and she carried it with her everywhere. And Gloria Swanson had her rose. Liberace would be just as much fun without his candelabra. You can say that that's his trademark, but why does he need his trademark? It's as if to say, "This is me; without the candlelabra I'm not me." And nobody thinks twice about this. The practice of this level of witchcraft is very common.

I'm not calling it real witchcraft, but there's a parallel. People say there's power in prayer. Prayer reestablishes your confidence, gives you courage and makes concrete your abstract, vague thoughts and feelings—and it works. Chants work this way too. Don't think of witchcraft as involving the devil; it's not a matter of good and evil forces. There's energy to tap, so tap it for whatever you will. It's not bad OR good.

You might not have enough psychic energy to influence other people in a subtle way, but you certainly have enough energy to influence yourself. Witchcraft is a way of disciplining your subconscious, so you can achieve success. Aside from the objects and chants, it is basically an exercise of the mind. Can anyone can teach himself to do it? Being a witch is a genetic thing, but anyone can work at the arts and powers of witchcraft for their own personal gain.

There is a psychic energy that not everybody shares. Everyone is NOT born equal, and not everybody develops this. You can learn the trade, the tools of witchcraft, just as you can learn how to paint; that won't immediately make you a great painter. It can be fun to belong to a choral group like the Sweet Adelines, but that doesn't make you a great operatic singer. Witchcraft is not a paint-by-the-numbers game that any child can do, although most children start out with the wild mental energy that witchcraft thrives on. We all have little secret feelings about what's going to take place, and once we free the cloudy mind and learn how to use it, we can not only see the future—which is very easy for a witch to do—but we can grasp it, control it, change it. The power is there, we know. All you have to do is pull it to the surface. And even if you never learn to change your enemy into a frog, witchcraft, like sex, is a pleasant way to pass the time.

# 3
# Spells and Chants

*"With the pricking of my thumb,
something evil this way comes,
Open Locks, Whoever Knocks..."*
William Shakespeare

    Handed down from generation to generation, witchcraft is rich in ritual, especially when it comes to love. The closely guarded secrets provide a spell for every lover who ever ached for fulfillment, a potion to persuade the reluctant, a chant to enforce the powers of the mind, and even recipes to vitalize the passions.

    The objects and words used in witchcraft are many and diverse, all calculated to work their own special magic, all tested and proven by their continued use from the huts in European villages of centuries ago to the voluptuous apartments of the modern era.

    Even beginners in witchcraft can practice these spells. However, the success of every sorcerer is virtually dependent on his or her confidence. Old witches say that a tiny clove of garlic sewn inside a small, heart-shaped piece of silk, attached with a gold pin to the left side of your undergarments, will act for confidence, protect you from the plague, ward off evil spirits and attract energetic lovers. It's worth a try.

According to the old views on witchcraft, everyone should have a lucky charm to protect him from evil forces. Usually it is a birthstone ring. There is a ritual, a spell, for preparing this ring.

## I. FULL-MOON RING

On the afternoon of the new moon fill a copper bowl with earth, and place it on a square of red silk in the center of a table. At 9 p.m. boil water in a cauldron or stainless steel pot, and cook the ring for nine full minutes. While the ring is boiling, place nine white taper candles around the copper bowl. Bury the ring in the earth. Light the candles, and as they blaze they will instantly act as agents to purify the earth inside the copper bowl.

The candles should flame brightly for 90 minutes, at the end of which time sprinkle three drops of olive oil over the copper bowl three separate times, nine drops in all. Each time chant, "My energies are a gift to the cosmos; my soul belongs to the wind. I am the cosmos; I am the wind." That makes you powerful forever. The ring must stay in the bowl until midnight of the night of the full moon, two weeks later. At that moment place the ring on your finger. Later, bury the bowl, the earth, the candles and the silk in a garden. Then you are ready to practice witchcraft.

From that moment forward you are protected, and nobody can ever steal the ring from you without coming to harm. Wear this ring at all times. Once you start being witchy, it's a full-time job, and you need protection at all times. Always wear your ring while casting spells. Always work a spell at the same hour of day and if possible in the same location, because it's the repetition of the spell that will insure the success of it.

## II. ISIS FULL-MOON RING

There is one variation on this chant: pledging the new sorcerer not to the cosmos in general, but to the Moon, which is said to influence the emotions of women—and indeed does, considering the menstrual calendar and the changes in feelings it brings about from cycle to cycle. Not even my great-grandmother remembered why variations in chants exist—it's just that witches always have done it one way or another.

Isis is the ancient goddess of the Moon whose magic, when all is lost and you have gone down and under, will charm you once again to even higher heights. Enchantresses who perform rituals in her name are granted special favors. She is queen of witchcraft, known for her sympathetic intervention into affairs of the heart. She has never turned her face from anyone who has called her name. For beginning sorcerers no attempt should be made to cast a spell, perform a ritual, work a charm, enchant or fascinate without the protection of the ring described, called a Full Moon Ring. The birthstone is said to offer the most protection. However, the stone that you associate with your moonsign is also highly effective. The chant variation is: "In the name of Isis, goddess of the Moon, I offer my energies as a gift of the cosmos; my soul belongs to the wind. I am the cosmos; I am the wind."

Witchcraft can be a comforting *modus operandi*. In spell casting, the ritual is performed in a forceful attempt to alter a moment in time, by creating a vibration within the environment that in turn will set into motion a series of events leading ultimately to the desired conclusion. Sorcery goes a giant step beyond mere positive thinking by generating situations demanding positive action, commitment.

If you would like some additional romantic action, with silver three times tap crystal, nine times ring a small clear bell, and daylong let a teapot gently whistle. But most effective of all is candle glow. "A home with candles burning brightly will be visited by sexy woodnymphs nightly."

In the beginning, herbs were used to placate gods. Man burned herbs to release pungent aromas meant to stimulate the senses of the deity and insure favors. Herbs have been included in food, baths, spells, closets, spell potions, medical treatments, magical rites and religious ceremonies. They have been used for emotion-elevators, decorations of the elevated, and dietetic inspiration; they have been expected to honor you, dry you out, fatten you up, make you strong, protect from harm, bring him back, break the tide, cure the plague, bring in money and inhibit infidelity. Ancient Greece bought courage with thyme, Romans cured drunkenness with parsley, and Charlemagne grew rosemary because it was known to fortify memory. The Bible says that dinner with herbs may be better where love is, but all witches know that love is frequently better when herbs are in the dinner.

## III. BLOOD CHARM

In Sicily certain modern segments of the youthful in-love society cling to a primitive belief that a few drops of blood from the the lady's finger mixed with the gentleman's hot *café royale* will bind them to eternity. So potent is the supposed spell that it is not considered necessary for the gentleman to know about it. It may be dangerous to capture a man in this way unless the lady truly loves him. She must beware; the spell binds them both, and it is not to be taken lightly. Many a frivolous sweetheart discovers that magic cannot be undone, and like the thumb, the enchanter, too, is stuck.

With control, witchcraft offers a beneficial outlet for creative energy. In the ancient craft all things are unified and related, and there is no chaos.

Any time you cast a spell you should be in a small area so you can control the atmosphere easily. Don't do this in the middle of a ball park because you cannot control all the vibrations in an area that large. You'll need a small room and a table top, preferably one used only for spellcasting. Most of the equipment you use should be new, and it's suggested that you use new equipment for each and every one of your spells, lest the associations connected with old things intervene. The new witch should get new candles, new bowls, new everything.

# Spells and Chants

Around the whole room sprinkle a circle of salt so that the magic act is protected inside. It's best to use coarse salt instead of the refined kind. Remain within the protection of the ring of salt for the entire length of the spell. If someone comes to the door while you're casting any spell, you should ignore it. If the telephone rings, ignore it. Try to set yourself up so you will have as little distraction as possible. Take the phone off the hook to insure no call. You want nothing to break the continuity of your concentration, and if any disturbance should happen, continue with your spell; don't get out of it. Stay right there and block out the sounds that you hear. You must attempt to do this. Even if you're not successful in the beginning, eventually you will be.

## IV. THE SEXUAL SEDUCTION SPELL

Here is the formula for the Sexual Seduction Spell:

1. Find a piece of paper that is pretty and pleasing to you.
2. On this paper, write your whole name: first, middle and last.
3. Under your name, write your lover's full name. (Always write your own name first, in order to maintain control. If your lover's name appears above yours, you will be dominated.)
4. Write down your lover's birthdate, followed by your own.
5. Draw a heart around the information.
6. Repeat the information, writing it directly over the original writing, three times. It will be indecipherable when you're through, and will look like plain scribbling.
7. When you have completed the writing, fold the paper as small as possible, and burn it in the flame of a red, or orange-red candle, until it is reduced to an ash. (You need a large red candle with a large base so that it can support the burning of this paper without falling to the table.)

8. While the paper burns, chant this incantation *three* times:
>Light the flame
>Bright the fire
>Red is the color
>Of desire

9. Repeat the entire process every day or night for nine consecutive days. That's considered one spell. After that you use it as needed to reinforce.

Most witches save the ashes from all of their spells in a special little box. The box, because it's been used for years, develops magical properties of its own and can be used as a lucky talisman to bring good luck. Don't just take the ashes and throw them out in the trash. You must treasure these things; they're potent.

## V. CHARMED SLEEP

Spellcasters use an enormous amount of energy, and in order to insure that the energy is restored, charmed sleep is essential. This is attained through a simple ritual. Place a desert turtle under your bed. Put fresh mint leaves inside your pillowcase and place a rose-tinted crystal glass filled with water next to your bed. Three bright yellow daffodils are set up at your window. Light three blue candles and let them flame for one hour while you're getting ready to go to bed. Then draw a protective white chalk circle around the bed. Once between the covers you say, "Sandoz" eight times. Sleep in the nude or it doesn't work.

Witchcraft hinges on desire, and the reason for this is that most people find it easy to become emotional about things they want, about things they love. It's difficult for them to become emotional about a dress or money. That's the whole key to it. Men who have made fantastic amounts of money do so because they can become aroused and emotionally turned-on with money. The average person can't. If you can get your emotions going you can accomplish anything. Don't think about what money might bring. You've got to understand very clearly that once you have the money, it will bring all the things you want to buy, so there's no point in wasting your energy thinking about the end results. Start by thinking about the money. Once you turn-on for money it will start coming to you. You eventually can arouse a desire for money once you learn how to trigger your emotions, but it takes practice. You must learn to project your emotional intensity in order to have it create the situation you want. The best way to do that is to begin with sex and love and build up slowly to money. Sex and love are easy for most people, because they naturally cause emotional energy.

When you like someone very much, when you're attracted to him, it shows. Something is transmitted by the force and power of the emotion. The thing to do now is feel that way about money or your job or your career—something other than love. Put the same forces to work, and when that happens, you get money. So you can use witchcraft for things other than love, but it takes a lot of work and is more difficult. It takes practice.

## VI. SPICE RUB

Egypt's elite were known for their superior sexual ability and spicy approach to life. They would rub a special spice and herb mixture all over their lover's body in order to increase sexual excitement. There is no way now to know if their success was due to spicy, aromatic inhalation or spicy outer rubitations. Here is the lover's magical spice and herb mixture: one teaspoon powdered cumin, the Greek and Turkish spice; one teaspoon powdered mace; teaspoon powdered sage; teaspoon powdered thyme; a pinch of rosemary; teaspoon of powdered cloves; teaspoon of powdered nutmeg and a tablespoon of powdered ginger. Grind them all together, and you have a very sexy spice. Use all new spices. Don't use anything you've got lying around the kitchen because that might impart something from a previous situation; also use new utensils. Never mix anything else in the utensils that you use for your sex spells.

A small, clear bell rung nine times will bring visitors from the outer world. A whistling teakettle insures helpful support from the other world, so you can keep a teakettle on a low flame and just let it gently whistle. This sets up the proper vibration to bring about things you want. What it actually does is constantly support your concentration and determination. It reminds you, fixes your idea firmly in mind. If you begin to think that that whistling teakettle on the kitchen stove is going to drive you wild, you're right; it will.

## VII. TRUE LOVE TEA

For beginners in sorcery, here is a very simple love tea to make: Every night for two hours, between 9 p.m. and 11 p.m., burn an orange-red candle—sort of coral color, not bright red and not clear orange. Light the candle and sip the tea. This is for people who are very lonely and want to establish an emotional relationship, a true love, with someone. It's a very tedious spell, but effective. The tea starts with any blend you like, spiked with nutmeg, rosemary, thyme, rosebuds, honey and lemon leaves, a small amount of each. This chemical combination has all the witching ingredients it takes for attracting a true love. Begin sipping True Love Tea on an odd number date: three, five, seven, nine, et cetera, and continue for six weeks, every night. It is for people who have been alone for a long time. You can repeat this spell many times if you want, but it takes six weeks so don't wear yourself out. Once you get the spell completed, you can reinforce it by having this tea, say, every Friday night. Friday is recommended because it's a Venus-ruled day and has to do with love activities.

You can also combine True Love Tea with the Sexual Seduction Spell (once you get the thing rolling), and do the two spells at the same time. You can even throw in an Emotional Bondage Spell, described later. There is also a love cake that's guaranteed to increase sexual vitality and to cure infidelity. It's an Italian love cake known for over 300 years. Updating the recipe so that it's easier than starting from scratch, it is possible

# Spells and Chants

to use the Bisquick muffin mix. First, fry crisp a half pound of Italian sweet sausage until practically all the oil is out of it. Then season it with ginger and add a half pound of very finely chopped candied fruits. Next, add about one quarter of a package of bittersweet chocolate chips, two cups of Bisquick, a half cup of brown sugar, one egg, three-fourths cup of milk, and one-fourth cup of black coffee. It's easiest to take the Bisquick, the milk, the egg, the sugar, the coffee and the ginger, and mix them all together. Add the sausage, then the fruit, and finally the chocolate. Bake until done in a 400 degree oven. The recipe makes 15 small love cakes. Feed the cakes to your husband or lover over the weekend, and it will keep him in line for the next month or so. You can achieve the same effect without the love cake, but it's very difficult, and you must sustain your confidence all the time. So, in case you weaken and doubt yourself, the cake takes over for you. You eat it, he eats it, and you can serve it to the whole family. It keeps everybody in line, but it's especially effective on your lover.

Once people start using witchcraft, they should become aware of the special dates in the year for casting spells. There are days when the position of the earth in relationship to the other planets and the sun allows for a more effective use of magnetic forces. There are special festival dates: February 2, April 30, August 1 and, of course, October 31. The other dates are not the same every year, because the earth doesn't come back to the same position, in relation to the sun every year on the same day. Very effective times are around March 21, the vernal equinox; June 21, the summer solstice; September 21, the autumnal equinox; and December 21, the winter solstice. Get a current calendar and find out the first day of spring; certain spells are cast the night before. Also important are the nights before the first day of summer, fall and winter. There seems to be more force to spells cast at these times. Another thing to watch is the moon. New and full-moon days are very effective for spellcasting. Use the new moon for beginnings and the full moon for endings—either for romance. The moon dates give you 24 good spell days a year. The special dates and festivals give you another eight. That's 32 good spell days a year, which ought to keep anybody hopping.

The new moon is when the moon is dark, and anything you do at the new moon should be something that you want quick results from because it's bound to happen in the next two weeks. By the time the moon is full you should get what you want. Usually the new moon spell is used for quick attractions. They're not days to use for your whole life-span project. Use the vernal equinox for the life pattern and the new moon for fun and games.

## VIII. THE MONEY INCREASE SPELL

Here's one that's fun, but it's not a moon spell: The Money Increase Spell. Cast this at one minute after midnight on any one of the special festival dates. You could do it at the new moon, too, but when you do the new moon money spell, it may help quickly to pay an overdue bill, but it's not going to be a life pattern. The festival dates are the best ones for that. At one minute after midnight on the festival date, you should have all set up: one gold candle, six green candles, and nine white candles. And, of course, salt. Place the gold candle in the center of the table and circle it with the six green candles. Then enclose these inside a circle of the nine white candles. Use the salt to pour a protective circle around the candles. Light the candles, and chant three times:

> Orbiting Jupiter,
> Trine the sun:
> Bring money on the run.

Your finances should begin to improve within 19 days. This is your lifelong money aspect, not the spell you do with the new moon for quick money. For quick money throw brand new coins into your house, from outside, on the day of the new moon, and let them roll wherever they will. Don't pick them up for the rest of the month. The chant is, "Money on the floor, money through the door." It's best to have mint-new coins from the bank, but it doesn't matter what the denominations. Remember, wherever they roll, don't touch them for the rest of the month. You don't have to go any further outside than far enough to put your back out of the front door so you're facing in when you throw the coins.

## IX. ORGIES

There's a special kind of energy derived from uniting with someone sexually, and a spellcaster uses so much energy that she needs a tremendous amount of uniting. I know one woman who participates in orgies regularly because she's a witch, and although I think it's weird, she doesn't seem to think it's strange at all. In order for a spell to be successful, a great deal of emotional energy must be generated, so an orgy, if done properly, can prime the pump. The best time to cast a spell would be moments before the orgy is consummated. That's when the atmosphere is charged with electrical-magnetic impulses and tends to promote success of the attempted spell. Some spellcasters insist that only orgies supply the type of excitement needed, and, of course, there are other spellcasters who just enjoy orgies. Any spell can be cast; the orgy just supplies the energy to do it, and supposedly fires you up. Witches usually don't waste orgies on little spells; they do big ones aimed at the whole life pattern. To break an old pattern and establish a new direction, they'll have an orgy in which all the witches cast spells.

But these are not the typical covens that everyone talks about, with 12 women and one man. There are a lot of women and a lot of men. Some witches who aren't group-minded will cast a spell before they get into bed nude with somebody. Frequently, the lover is innocent and does not understand that he is being used for a spellcast. Often, though, he is aware. I mean, at a time like that, what kind of a person would cast a spell? It would have to be a witch. You've got to have all the paraphernalia dragged out and set up before you are ready to climb into bed. Usually this type of thing is better when both people involved are experienced spellcasters who may no longer need props but are able to project a thought strongly enough without candles and incense and bells ringing—although of course they still can be utilized.

## X. CANDLE MAGIC

It is well-known that certain colored candles stand for certain things.

The colors mean something to most people who deal with this type of thing. White candles are always used for inspiration, increase in knowledge or an inner solution for a particular problem. If you want inspiration to hit, light a white candle.

Blue candles are protection against evil, and they will put a magnetic field around you if you light one. Many who set out on a trip take a blue candle along and light it every night to keep themselves safe during their journey.

A yellow candle represents spiritual love. The kind of love, perhaps, between two people with a tremendous age difference and no sexual attraction but a similarity of ideas and exchange of thoughts. It's not the flesh and blood kind of love.

An orange-red candle is for sexual activity. This is the color that traditionally has been used for this purpose. It has to do with sexual seduction and sexual attraction spells.

Green candles are for all new beginnings, such as starting a new job or making new friends. Some witches even use green candles to keep a relationship going, because it gives another aspect to it: newness. Green is also especially good for financial security.

Black candles are for evil wishes. If you want to tap evil forces, harm someone, or just to gain control of a rough situation without necessarily harming anybody, use the black candle.

The purple candle is for contact with the spirit world, and it's good for giving psychic readings. If you want to get messages from somebody who has departed, use a purple candle.

The silver candle is to stop slanderous gossip about yourself, your friends or family. The gold candle projects good health.

Don't fool with a red candle. It's beyond sex. It's awfully primitive, and it's best not to mess with it. Not if you're a novice, anyway. Leave the red candle to full-fledged witches. Stick to orange-red for sex. It's all you'll be able to do to control the results of that!

To alter circumstances you must be intense, emotional, self-motivated and capable of obsession. That's the only way it can work. And you must understand that once you cast a spell you've set into motion vibrations that can never be erased. They can never be stopped. Something's going to happen. Once in motion, there's no return, so you must be very brave. You may be able to alter the conclusion a bit, but things will never remain the same; they are no longer what they were. That's another difference between witchcraft and positive thinking. Positive thinking doesn't put you in danger. In witchcraft you make a complete commitment. It's like jumping off a building. You can't go halfway down and then say "Uh-oh." You must keep going.

## XI. THE SELF-FASCINATION SPELL

Here is a spell that delves into the very heart of witchcraft, creating power inside you by sharpening your faculties and bringing them to bear on the most important thing in your life: you. In order to increase control over others, the Self-Fascination Spell must be performed regularly. Strip nude in front of a mirror in a dark room. Light one candle of any color except red. (Only if you're already very powerful can a red one be used.) Raise your arms high over your head and rhythmically sway from left to right as you repeat your first name 99 times, continuing to sway while you're repeating your name. The best way to do this is to write your name 99 times, and then read it off, so you can keep track. Some spellcasters use 99 flower petals to keep track of their counting. For each petal you touch, say your name.

It must be an exact count to 99. When you stop swaying at the count of 99, become very dynamic and tense, much the same as when you're doing isometric exercises. Clench your fists, stiffen your muscles, brace yourself all over and repeat three times, "I control. I am the power." Blow out the candle and it's over. Cast this spell on Tuesdays and Fridays for three months, and it will never fail to improve your life. It's good for the waistline, too.

A few decades ago a popular psychologist had everyone around the world marching to their mirror every morning saying, "Every day in every way, I am getting better, and better, and better." Well, I tell myself things in the mirror, too, all the time. I've done it all my life. I look in the mirror and tell myself what everything is about. Seeing yourself puts you more in contact with yourself. We all live up in the back of our heads somewhere, but if we can become accustomed to looking at ourselves, thinking aloud, we get to know ourselves better. And what we know, we control.

Mirrors are very important in witchcraft. There's another thing single people can do with a mirror on Halloween. Go out to where you can see the moon and put your back to it so the reflection of its light will fall on the mirror. Then light a candle and put it in front of your face so you can see your face with the moon behind you. Over your shoulder will appear an image of the person you are going to marry.

## XII. EMOTIONAL BONDAGE SPELL

If your partner is sexy but projects little emotional warmth, then you must try the Emotional Bondage Spell. It's a dangerous spell, as frequently the conjurer gets conjured. You must be certain that you really want him. Never bind anybody to you merely for kicks, and never, ever use the Emotional Bondage Spell where there is little or no sexual compatibility, because you will be stuck with that person forever.

Light three candles, one yellow, one orange, AND, if you're really strong, one red. If you don't think you can handle it, use just an orange-red candle. Surround a photograph of the love object with the three candles and 47 yellow blossoms. Then say

47 times, "We are one, we are one, we are one," and gaze at the photo for nine full minutes after you say this. Then sip True Love Tea and ring a bell three times. If you really want to be tricky, you can take a few drops of your blood and drop it into his food. That's a cincher.

If fooling around with candles makes you feel odd, consider this: Millions and millions of people, for century after century, spent their most thoughtful moments staring at the tongues of fire from candles and torches and, before that, campfires. And untold millions, attending church ceremonies, were conditioned by flickering candlefire as they made their strongest efforts to contact the supernatural, God. Odd? Not a bit. If thought has any force beyond our own small persons, then no greater communication with the thought energies of millions could be approached than through the common human fascination with controlled fire.

## XIII. THE COLEOPTEROUS CHARM

One charm that will have a catalytic effect upon all personal relationships, and will project a romantic aura about the charmer that love objects will find irresistably exciting, is the ancient Coleopterous Charm. Since Cleopatra's time, the coleopterous (beetle) has been a symbol for occult beginnings, germination force, power, birth, life and death—and, above all, magic. Enchantresses insist that a Coleopterous Charm will insure a very satisfying love life. The charm should increase sexual vitality, attract many healthy, vibrant love relationships, encourage fidelity, prolong romantic desire and protect the clandestine. For all that, certainly this charm is worth considerable effort. Cleopatra knew how to prepare a Coleopterous Charm; however, the exact preparation she used has been lost. She carried it to her grave.

The Ironclad Beetle Love Charm is the most successful Coleopterous Charm since Cleopatra's. Take one live, ironclad beetle and wrap it into a small square of red silk. Place this small packet inside a tiny wooden box that has been painted bright red. Now cover the packet with one half cup of dried rosebuds. Close the lid and seal the box with wax. Place the box and its contents in the northeast corner of your home and light a tapered purple candle. Chant, "Coleopterous Magnificent, Coleopterous Blessed, Coleopterous Beloved, Coleopterous Eternal." It is not considered important if the beetle dies.

The way to a man's heart is through his stomach, the saying goes, but mix in a little witchcraft just to be sure. Witches know that if you add *melissa officionalis* (lemon balm) to your fellow's bath, his straying will stop; he'll stay where he oughter; and a bit of anise added to the cake makes any tired old lover turn into a rake.

Figs, dates and eggs are supposed to be the sexiest foods. Oysters and fish, too. Fish is very high in vitamin E, which may have some effect on sexual activity. When a man is having difficulty getting a woman pregnant, doctors often advise increasing the vitamin E intake for her and the man, so there must be something vital in it. The Chinese eat seahorse, and they consider this the ultimate stimulant for sexual desire and potency.

As for beverages, use your imagination. You might put three drops of female blood into his coffee, or try True Love Tea spiked with booze. As an icebreaker, a whiskey sour spiced with just a dash of cumin might do. Here's a hot one: Take instant coffee and heat a cup of milk for each cup of coffee; use a half spoon of instant coffee and a half spoon of chocolate—not cocoa —a teaspoon of sugar, a dash of nutmeg and a cinnamon stick. Rum, if desired.

There are dozens and dozens of spells and recipes, of course, most of them very old. But accomplished, modern-day witches, if they know the significance of the objects and process involved, often create their own. Perhaps you feel somebody has harmed you. You want revenge. One way to accomplish this is to mail, every day for nine days, the same type of flower—no return address, nothing but a flower for nine days in a row. That causes everything they have done to you to go back to them. That's a century-old spell. Here is a fairly new one, based on the same principle: If you want to get rid of somebody, to make them go away, procure some soil from another state, and mail them a little bit every day for nine days. That will pull them toward that direction.

Or, supposing you have used the powerful card spell to hex somebody. Draw the circle layout as described in Chapter Four, and make a symbol of each of the cards you have placed to effect the hex, K for king, J for jack, et cetera. Mail one diagram a day for nine days. It will drive them crazy, if nothing else, to get that incomprehensible thing in the mail for nine days running.

Trim your hair a quarter of an inch every new moon, and it will grow in thick and luxurious. Start a new business at the last quarter, the week before the new moon. This is the most dynamic period. But to begin a new love affair, it's best to pick the quarter or the week just before the full moon, in order to have the right emotional influences.

Aside from the seasonal influences and festival dates mentioned earlier, there are some days of the week that are better than others for spellcasting, and there are specific reasons why. Saturday is a good day for casting spells connected with money, and Friday is good for emotion, but Wednesday is good for most witch spellcasts. In fact, Wednesday is the best day of the week for witch spells, because Wednesday is more involved with the intellect. We are not so much moved by passion and emotion; we're very cool, and when you are casting a spell you must be able to turn on an emotional intensity, but only enough to support some very clear thinking. It isn't good to be passionate and aroused and a bit dizzy all at the same time. Wednesday is the best clearheaded day. If you've got a case in court, for instance, it would be very good if you could get it on a Wednesday. It's that kind of day.

The days of the week are named after planets, in all languages. Sunday, naturally, is derived from the sun, and Monday is moon day. In foreign countries, the same practice is followed: It's a global custom. The Chinese god, Tui, was a war god, and although our war god, Mars, comes from the Romans, we named Tuesday after Tui. The French use Mardi in honor of

Mars. The Spanish and French named Wednesday after Mercury, but we use the Germanic "Wodensday." Woden was the counterpart of the god Mercury. Thursday is Thor's day. Thor was the god who was comparable to Jupiter and although the French and Spanish named their Thursday after Jupiter, we stick to Thor. Thor and Jupiter were the same gods in different parts of the world.

Friday comes from Venus but we use the German "Freitag," the equivalent goddess. Saturday is Saturn's day.

It is not only witches who set aside special days. There are certain traditional days to do certain things; all sorts of tricky things that most women know about. A Sunday marriage is blessed and, of course, this may be why so many more people get married on Sunday than on any other day. Monday marriages are likely to face great ups and downs and changes because of the connection with the phases of the moon. Tuesday weddings mean arguments and a bit of inconstant behavior. (It's Mars' day, which means a lot of strife and trouble and difficulties.) Wednesday is based on commercial, level-headed values, control over emotions. Thursday is pretty good if you want to have a swinging affair and a lot of unexpected money coming in. Friday, being a Venus-ruled day, can be a day of sorrow. Lovers face many tragic moments and they reach a point of separation and then make up again. It's a very emotional day. Saturdays are for practical people.

For example, two people marrying on Wednesday, Mercury's day, might do so for appearances or for commercial gain. A homosexual and a lesbian, for instance, might marry on Wednesday. On the other hand, Saturn's people, those who marry on Saturday, generally stick to their commitment, sometimes against all odds. They might end up hating each other, even become sexually incompatible, yet still they usually stay together.

## XIV. UNWANTED LOVER SPELL

Speaking of sex and war, there is a Tuesday-oriented spell that comes in handy for fiery young ladies. An experienced spellcaster who has increased her animal magnetism and sexual attraction frequently runs into the problem of having too many lovers. Now she needs a spell to get rid of an unwanted lover. As she is totally responsible for having created this irresistible attraction, she can also break the spell and get rid of the old lover to make way for the new.

You must call on Nai-no-kami, the Japanese god of earthquakes. Begin on the third Tuesday of the month, and at 9 p.m. enter into a quiet area; the only light must be the flame from one large, black candle. Ring a clear bell three times, and on parchment paper draw the symbol to. the Sun, the Moon and the planets (see Figure I). Stain the parchment with eight juicy seeds of a pomegranate, then completely burn the parchment in the flame. Take the ashes and touch them to your forehead. Remain gazing quietly at the flame a full three minutes, then shout out, as loudly as you can, his name: Nai-no-kami!

Make up nine small packets, putting in each one some of the ashes from the parchment, three cloves, a soft grey feather and some sand. Extinguish the black candle. Place the packets into envelopes and seal them with sealing wax. The next day at 3 p.m., and each day until all nine are mailed, post a packet to the unwanted lover. At the end of that time, or before, he'll stop bothering you, and you'll be free for other love affairs.

## XV. DREAM SPELL

Would you like to visit a cherished friend while traveling to a dream dimension? There's a variation of the Charmed Sleep Spell for this: Draw the light, chalk, protective circle around your bed; place a large turtle under the bed and three fresh mint leaves in your pillowcase. Before retiring, light three blue candles, and let them flame for one hour. Blow out the candle, ring a bell once, and nine times whisper, "Orpheus, Orpheus, Orpheus," et cetera.

Practicing witches, as we indicated, are able to create their own spells and design them for specific situations once the idea of how they work is mastered. When I was younger and more adventurous, I would set up all sorts of things to try and make something happen. Actually I was learning to condition my subconscious so thoroughly through these spells that it projected the thought and attracted me toward the thing that I wanted, however removed it was from the spell itself.

I did many little silly things. For example, I decided once that I wanted to meet a certain big celebrity. I put it in my mind that this should be done, and that once I met him many other things in my life would fall into place and begin to happen.

I performed a ritual to set up a series of events that would lead to my meeting this powerful man. After that I never went anywhere without running into him. His wife would sit next to me at the Hollywood Bowl, or I'd walk through a door and he'd be coming out. He looked startled each time, probably because I was ready to meet him. Every time he came through a door I'd react with a very strong force that probably would not have been there had I not performed the ritual, so naturally he reacted to my reaction, and before I knew it he was saying, "Hello." I didn't deliberately go anyplace where he would be. I didn't do anything physical that would make it happen. It just happened.

As for the ritual itself, I lit a candle in a darkened area, then burned incense. If you can get all your senses going at the same time you make more of an impression on your subconscious for the thing you want. I hypnotized myself into feeling that I was surrounding this man with myself and calling him into my sphere of being. I think we are all a mass of energy, and we really have no clearly defined end. Where does my body end and the air around me begin? At which point do the molecules no longer unite into a separate entity? I don't understand the principle involved in what keeps me together so I don't understand the natural law that would prevent my leaving my body and surrounding another person, and because I am stupid I am able to do it. I can absorb things and situations. I begin feeling as if an octopus form were coming out of me, and I can surround and hug everything I want. As long as I can sustain the sensation of surrounding something, it's mine.

## XVI. YOUR WORD OF POWER

Even a novice at witchcraft can take some steps to individualize some parts of the practice. You can choose your own Word of Power, and each morning when you arise, say it before you even set your feet on the floor. Here's how to find your Word of Power: Get a dictionary and put it on your lap. Turn it sideways, upside down and every which way, without looking at it, so you don't know, literally, which end is up. Insert your finger into the book with your eyes closed and move it around until you get the urge to stop. When the urge strikes, stop. Your finger will locate your magic word. It's important that the word be chosen on the first try and adopted permanently. It's your own magic word. Chance brought it to you. Utter the word each morning. Now you are controlling chance.

Witches frequently use books to give themselves psychic readings, as well. This is done by selecting a book that is meaningful to you, but has a broad scope. That is, a book of quotations, perhaps, or poetry, or even a dictionary. Almost anything but a novel, which doesn't provide a broad enough range of words. Make up a pattern, wildly, saying the first thing that comes into your head, like: On the fortieth page, fifteenth sentence, and the third word over, my message begins. Then pick another, and another, and another, until you have a predetermined number of words, say 25. The words won't be in the right word order, but there will be a message there that applies to your life.

My mother used to do this all the time. She had a special set of favorite spellcast books, and when I'd come into the room looking troubled, she'd go to them. Her finger would move around at random, and she'd begin writing down words. It was great! When I was worried about a lover, for instance, she would even come up with his correct name.

But you must make your plan ahead of time so that you are

committed to the words you come to. What actually happens is that your subconscious moves into action and allows you to read into the words something your subconscious powers want to tell you, so it's a message from an intelligence greater than your conscious mind.

If you're starting a new relationship, and you're wondering about it, try the dictionary. I remember once I met a man and wondered what kind of relationship we'd have. I used the dictionary, and the first word I blindly chose was: nitroglycerine. It turned out to be that kind of a romance, too! I got the word three times in a row after juggling the book around so much that my finger never should have hit the same place twice.

The secret is to set a code and stick with it from the first. Now you can tell not only your own fortune every day, but anybody else's you wish.

# 4

# The Card Spell—
# The Biggest Spell of All

> *"When the light goes down in evening
> and the crab is on the crawl"*
> *(Gloom Glob Vendors)*
> Louise Huebner

Witches are always being contacted by people who are eager to know their fortune, what destiny has in store for them. And, because witches tend to be psychic, often they can get impressions of the future that prove true. But this is not the chief business of a witch: A witch doesn't care much about peering into the future to see what destiny has in store; a witch occupies herself, mainly, with tampering with that destiny, causing things to happen in the future.

Of all the spells, there is one that can sweep over every portion of our lives to solve single problems or alter the entire life pattern, but it is a difficult spell and requires study. It requires 12 circles, each with a different meaning in relation to the phases of your life, and a deck of playing cards. Not Tarot cards. Everyone interested in fortunetelling has heard much about the supposedly mystic Tarot deck. The Tarot deck is nonsense. Through the centuries, any meaning it may ever have had has been lost and corrupted. Through the generations it has changed form hundreds of times. You might as well make up your own meanings for the cards. So use regular cards, but you must use a brand new pack.

Cards came into being originally as a means of looking into the future. The games came later, evolving from fortunetelling. With the witchcraft system, you can not only look into the future, but change the parts of it you don't like. Fate is your slave.

This is a very secret method of casting spells by cards. It has been handed down from one witch to another for many generations—six in my family—but usually a witch would only give this knowledge to a member of her own bloodline and would not turn it over even to a witch from another family tie. Its exclusiveness should be respected, and it should be used with caution. As cards were originally used only for magical purposes, there developed, way back in antiquity, a method of casting spells by setting a certain card in a particular position in a special circle pattern. Each card signified a particular thing and, because of its position, it would make the thing happen. Use this method to interpret what your future intends. You can also change your future by manipulating the cards in a certain way.

You will learn how to position the cards and what the meaning is for each of the positions. Draw twelve circles, in a circle, like the numbers on a clock big enough to set cards in. Each of these circles represents a particular department of your life. (See frontispiece.)

The first circle of the card spell has to do with you personally, your ego, your personality, what you do with yourself alone and separate from all other contacts. It has nothing to do with your family or your partner; it's you alone facing the world.

The second circle has to do with your natural resources. It is involved with where you go, the source of your strength. So, the second circle concerns your storehouse, your supplies and your money.

The third circle governs your immediate neighborhood, your very close neighbors. If, of course, you are in a position of government where a large area is connected with what you do,

# The Card Spell—The Biggest Spell of All

then the neighborhood can be your city, or your state. But if you are an ordinary citizen and have nothing to do with the government and nothing to do with world affairs, the neighborhood is just your block and the other people who live on it. Another part of its meaning is cousins. It doesn't have to do very much with sisters and brothers, unless the sisters and brothers should be a great distance away. If they live close by, they don't come into that circle; only your cousins come in it, and sometimes uncles and aunts, your relatives slightly removed from your own house.

The fourth circle has to do with your background. For instance, if you are away from your parents' home, the fourth circle would indicate your home town. It also indicates your inheritance and what you gain from the past—anything that might come down to you from another generation. If you are dealing with worries about whether or not you're going to be remembered in a will, the fourth circle is important.

The fifth circle has to do with romance only in terms of a creative outlet. It has much to do with creativity, and so in this respect it can also cover offspring—including books, poems, paintings, babies, romances, anything creative. it could be horse racing. This circle covers anything where you risk yourself in connection with something you're creating. Usually, though, it has to do with romance and love affairs.

The sixth circle has to do with your unavoidable responsibility—where it's not possible for you to escape; that which you really don't believe you have control over. You may actually have control over it, and probably do, but you don't believe it. It also covers your health, working conditions if you are not your own boss, and government service. It even covers your duty towards small pets: responsibility toward things you must take care of.

The seventh circle has to do with partnership. Now mostly this means marriage, but it also covers any kind of partnership, such as your agent, your manager, or a 50–50 investment partnership. Any situation where you and the other individual are considered equal is included in the seventh circle. It also has to do with how you appear to the outer world and what people think about you; so in the card spell, if you want to include your appearance and reputation, the seventh circle would be very important.

The eighth circle, coming as it does next to the seventh circle, means the same to the seventh as the second circle means to you; that is, it deals with other persons' natural resources. It's their storehouse and supply. Their money. And this can cover with insurance, taxes, and money that you get in a will. It also deals with sex, because it covers what the other person is offering you as opposed to what you have to offer him. In general, it's what you get from another person—or what you exchange.

The ninth circle has to do with expansion of yourself, and that could be either in travel, in thought, or in a religious experience or some form of idealism. It's where you leave yourself and offer yourself up to another cause or person. Usually that type of thing has to do with your philosophy, rather than sex and love. It's too abstract an area.

As opposed to the fourth, which was your base of operation, the tenth circle might be pictured as your roof, your cover, your prestige in the world, your power. It concerns your goals, when you do all the things that you're intending to do and how you can make good in your career. But it also, indirectly, has to do with people and authority over you. As the fourth circle had to do with people in your background, the tenth circle deals with the people you are trying to reach, so it can be the area dealing with your ambition.

The eleventh circle, you should notice, is directly opposite the fifth circle, which is the creative expression of yourself. The eleventh circle, being opposite the fifth, is what you reach because of that creative expression. If your creative expression is the writing of a book, the eleventh circle would indicate whether or not you were published or whether you were someone who just wrote for yourself and never were in print. In a love affair, the eleventh circle deals with what kind of relationship will be sustained from that love affair taking place. If you have children, the eleventh circle shows what they will attain and what kind of personalities they will have. So when you want to affect

## The Card Spell—The Biggest Spell of All

friends, lovers, publishers, and so on, you would deal to the eleventh circle.

The twelfth circle is the one that is immediately adjacent to the first, and this is your subconscious beside its hidden activities. If you're having a love affair, the twelfth circle would show whether or not it was a secret one or an open one. It's all the undercover part of your life. It also involves the undercover of people around you and their relationship to you. It's the slanderous side of your life, the secrets, the spies, the enemies, the attacks that you are not prepared for. Also it may concern mysterious illnesses that people have that might be chronic, the sort that eats away at them and never comes out in the open like a full-blast appendix operation—a chemical imbalance in their body, for instance, or something that nobody can diagnose. And the twelfth circle has to do with anything that may be keeping you imprisoned; but the twelfth circle is your subconscious, so it can open up into a beautiful area too, depending upon how you use your subconscious strength.

Once you learn the significance of the twelve circles, the next thing to do is choose a spellcasting time each week. You can only do this once a week; you cannot do it every day, and even if you just want to do it for readings, you still must limit yourself to once a week. Wednesday night is considered best for cards. Wednesday is ruled by Mercury and it has to do with inspiration and insight, so most witches utilize that evening for card spellcasting.

Astrology devotees will recognize in the circles' pattern a debt to their planetary lore, a common influence. True, but it doesn't mean that if you know astrology that enables you to become a witch. Most reputable witches can do just about anything, and they are well-informed on astrology. My family has three generations of astrologers, but six generations of witches as far back as we can trace.

The cards are most important. Shuffle the cards and cut them in three stacks, then put the stacks one on top of the other. Take the first twelve cards from the top to give yourself a fortune reading. The meaning of the card in relationship to the meaning of the circle gives you a picture of what is about to happen. You start with circle number one and place the cards around, one to a circle, to see what's going to happen to you in the future.

Now, if you want to cast a spell, cut the cards in three stacks, spread the deck face up, and then go through the 52 cards and choose what you want to have happen. You place only the chosen cards in the various circles that apply and then surround the circle of twelve with salt. The cards will have to stay on the pattern all week. They can not be moved. You also need candle protection all week.

Light a blue candle in the center of the circle of cards. Don't worry about burning all day while you are away; it doesn't have to burn all day long, particularly when you are not present. A candle has its catalytic effect on the atmosphere and you in one second a day. The minute or hour it is lit will reinforce what is happening while you cast the spell or make the reading, but just light it each day at the same time.

You must become familiar with what each circle represents and what each card represents, and, as with everything, it's best to become creative and blend these aspects. Learn to understand what it means when the Ten of Hearts falls into the third circle and it happens to touch a King of Clubs. You must know what the circles and the cards mean, because you must blend them to suit the facts in your own life, past and future. Only you know these. You must interpret things to fit your own life, because this is a very unique spell. How much your own psyche can tolerate will have to determine whether you put one card in one section or two cards in two sections . . . and whether or not you use twelve cards to cast the spell or all the cards in the deck. But you've got to be very sure you can control, understand and sustain the meaning of the spell, or you might be creating a spell for yourself that isn't what you intended it to be. It might be too much for you—or not enough.

It's best to start out very simply until you become adept at the spellcasting. Try at first with just one card in one department, because you know for sure what one card will mean in a particular section. When you get used to that, and when you see that you are gaining power and are beginning to understand the magic, then you can start expanding a little more and creating intricate patterns. Begin very safely and securely and see what happens.

Another move recommended for beginners, until they have mastered the ability of remembering the picture of the card layout for the spell they have cast is this: Once the card spell has been cast, draw a diagram of it, all twelve circles, indicating the cards that have been placed in the various circles. Carry this around with you and even sleep on it. Look at it as often as possible, studying it; this diagram, this spell, represents something you want, and you will be imbedding it in your own mind and causing yourself to act in accordance with achieving your desires.

Now you must learn the meanings of the cards, and this will take time, but the following list is here for ready reference until you have absorbed it all. You'll quickly recognize which cards represent the key people in your life, and which cards influence the main situations in your life, but there are always subtleties to become aware of, new situations popping up, and new people arriving on the scene—even if you have to make them arrive—so the whole deck can be important to everyone. Here is what the cards mean.

Ace of Hearts is traditionally a romantic card, but it deals with love versus sex. It has no other connotation except love. It's a general card. Usually, if it's representing an individual, it would be a man in his forties, a muscular type, not thin or a fat man, but a well-built man.

The King of Hearts is love. He could be light but he's not necessarily a blond, fair-skinned, blue-eyed person. He probably has light brown hair (The King of Diamonds is a real blond.) If the King of Hearts were set in the first circle, it would indicate that a man fitting that description had love for you or would be having a very personal contact with you soon. If placed in the second circle, you would be getting money from that man. In the third circle, you would meet that man in your neighborhood.

In the fourth, someone of that description would come to visit your home very soon. In the fifth, you'd be having an affair with him. In the sixth, he might be someone who has a connection with you, sort of a fated meeting—a close contact you'd meet through your working conditions or maybe just someone you met by flukey events. Seventh circle: You're soon to marry a man of that type, or a man of that type would want to be involved with you on a permanent level, not just an affair. Eighth circle, of course, has to do with sex relationship or strong attraction to a man of that type. Ninth circle, you might meet a man like that on a trip; it could also indicate a teacher or a doctor or a minister fitting that description for whom you would have a romantic interest. The tenth circle, you would either go to work for somebody who looked like that, or, if you have an affair with somebody who looks like that, he may soon become very successful and his career would improve very rapidly. He would be a man of importance in the community. If it's the eleventh circle, this person has a very good feeling toward you, and besides being your lover, you're also very friendly; it's a good, healthy, long-term relationship. If it's in the twelfth circle, you're having a secret affair with him.

Queen of Hearts, if you're a man, is the counterpart of the King of Hearts. It would be to a man what the King of Hearts is to a woman. But if you are a woman, the Queen of Hearts would represent your mother-in-law. It has to do with a woman who is not just a girl, so it's a womanly relationship you have, with a relative, for instance. It also has to do with passion. It can be used as a passion card, having no connection with male or female. If you want to cast a spell and put the Queen of Hearts in the fifth circle, that would trigger a passionate situation.

The Jack of Hearts is a younger lover, but it also could be the one you're engaged to, or it could be just a man of 40. But as the King of Hearts was a new man in your life, the Jack of Hearts is a man you are already involved with, and he could be any age.

Ten of Hearts is a very fortunate romantic card. It's so overpowering, emotionally, that if you put it in the second

## The Card Spell—The Biggest Spell of All

circle, it could even break up a romance because it's so potent. Put the Ten of Hearts in the seventh circle, in your fifth too, but keep it away from the money circle because this one is a little too potent. Put it up in the tenth, in the twelfth, the fifth or the seventh. But keep it away from the other ones. And keep it out of the third house, too. You certainly don't want a cousin to feel this way about you.

Nine of Hearts is your philosophical card. It's a protective card. If you were having an affair and you wanted to be sure that you weren't discovered, you would cast a spell by putting the Nine of Hearts in the twelfth circle, and that would insure a protection around your affair. If you want to protect any situation, stick that nine of Hearts in; of course, if the Nine of Hearts should fall into a particular circle during a reading, you know that that area is particularly protected and under good-luck influences.

Eight of Hearts is money through love. How you interpret this depends on what kind of business you're in. Money through love could also represent someone who is selling love items, and I imagine that perfume, cosmetics and jewelry would come under that heading, as well as prostitutes. Or it could mean that because something about you is appealing, it might bring money into your life, and that means love of other people for you in whatever way you want to interpret it.

Seven of Hearts is the marriage card. It also deals with the seventh circle of your life, so if it is placed, say in the tenth circle, it could mean marriage to someone who is very powerful. In the fourth circle, it would be marriage to a man or a woman who had a good heritage, a lot of security—maybe from a very good family, very many generations of a good name. If it's in the third, it might be marriage to somebody in the neighborhood, or even marriage to a relative, a distant cousin. If it's in the second, a tremendous amount of money is coming to you personally because of the marriage. If the Seven of Hearts is in the fifth circle, it could be a love affair with a married man or woman, and most likely that's what it is. It also can indicate a new romance that could lead to marriage, or that the love affair would be converted into marriage. The Seven of Hearts means marriage.

Six of Hearts means some emotional disturbances, maybe a problematic situation having to do with your love interest. So if the Six of Hearts is in the twelfth circle, it could mean that you were having a secret affair, and there would be a little flurry of scandal around you. If it were in the seventh you'd consider it a difficulty with your marriage mate or an emotional outburst with your business partner. If it were put in the third circle, you might touch off an emotional upset with your close neighbors or a cousin. If someone is having a secret love affair and you know about it, but not too many people do, and if you want to break them up, then to cast a spell you put the Six of Hearts in the twelfth circle to cause difficulty in their love affair. Any place that you want to kick up a little fuss, where you want trouble or a problem, you put the Six of Hearts.

Five of Hearts is the romantic card. It indicates flirtations of the sort that you have at parties, nightclubs or dances. If you wanted to stir up a romantic involvement, you could put the Five of Hearts in the fifth circle and maybe trigger a meeting with someone in a situation that could eventually lead to a love affair, but starts off with gaiety and fun and games. Sometimes it has to do with one-night stands, when you meet someone and have a brief moment with them, and then move on to someone else. If you want that, that's what the Five of Hearts will give you.

The Four of Hearts is a very stable plan for fulfilment. It has to do with actual courtship, engagements, friendship. If you want to put the Four of Hearts in your eleventh circle, that would give someone that you've been friendly with for a long time a nice warm feeling toward you. That would be a good way to begin the thing. In a spell for money, you could put the Four of Hearts in the tenth circle, if you want your boss to notice you and have a favorable reaction toward you. Put the *Five* of Hearts in the seventh circle to stimulate your husband; don't bother with the Four of Hearts, because he's already been through that with you; furthermore, don't bother with the Four in the twelfth house, because first you want to get his interest before you have a secret affair.

Three of Hearts has to do with things that are emotional and pleasing to you, like your hobbies or going to the theater. Say you haven't been out for a long time with your husband; you want to interest him in going out to dinner and going to the theater. Put the Three of Hearts in the seventh circle. It's the kind of card you'd put in the eleventh section, too, for activity with members of your own sex. It's a fun, friendly card. However, if in readings it should fall in the twelfth circle, it means that somebody, maybe a cousin, aunt or uncle, or somebody in your neighborhood, is spreading mean and vicious stories about you.

The Two of Hearts, the deuce, is very lucky; it's a wild card. It's the card that would trip up fate and destiny. Throw it pretty much anywhere you want to have something unexpected happen, to keep things moving. It's not too great a card to put in the seventh circle, because you don't want things to be too erratic in your partnerships. It is a good card to throw in the fifth circle. For luck, you might throw it in the money section to get a beautiful gift from a lover.

Ace of Diamonds is a fantastic financial windfall, and anywhere that you want this to hit is a good place to stick it. Wherever it falls by itself would determine the direction from which this windfall would arrive. Of course, if you want to have tremendous prestige, and if you're not dealing just with money but with your personal reputation, put it in the first circle. If you want to be married to someone like an actor or a politician or a writer, someone who has achieved worldwide fame, put it in the seventh circle. You don't want to fool around with having it in the fifth, because if you're having a love affair it's sometimes best for your lover not to be a well-known person. It could lead to difficulty. And don't put it in the twelfth circle because any secret affair would blow up into a scandal. It is a good card to stick in somebody else's twelfth circle to mess them up a little bit. It's a dynamic, powerful card, and by itself it means just plain good luck.

King of Diamonds is a very dignified male. He might be a lawyer who's got several other lawyers working for him, a man who's achieved some kind of recognition in his work. It also could indicate that you have a legal reason for having contact with a man of this type. It could signify divorce in the seventh circle. You've got to be very creative in your interpretations. This card, for example, varies so extremely that it could mean a divorce or it might mean that you are going to marry, depending upon your circumstances. If you are unhappily married, and if the King of Diamonds falls in the seventh circle, that could indicate one of you is thinking about divorce. If you're not married and the King of Diamonds comes in the seventh, it might mean that you are going to marry a lawyer. In the tenth it might be that you yourself will achieve tremendous recognition and dignity in the work you do. It has to do with dignity, and it has to do with reputation and long-standing situations.

Queen of Diamonds is the female version of the King of Diamonds. It also has to do with any woman who is over 35. Also, if you are a married man, it could indicate the "other woman" in your life. If you're a woman and the Queen of Diamonds falls in the seventh circle, it might indicate that your husband's having an affair. It would not be just a boyish affair, but one that had more of a permanent hold on him, a tricky thing to break up. The Queen of Diamonds has to do with a concept of time. Most witches have noted that it means either three days, three weeks, or three months, because the card has to do with seasons. If you are involved in a situation and want to know when it will reach its conclusion, deal a reading; if the Queen of Diamonds shows up your situation may be resolved next season.

Jack of Diamonds represents a younger man, and also has to do with improved business conditions. If it's in the first circle, there would be tremendous personality gains. You wouldn't be selling potatoes or merchandise of any sort, you'd be selling yourself in a situation. If you're an actor or actress, put the Jack of Diamonds in the first circle to win tremendous gains through your own personality. If you're an unmarried woman, placing the Jack of Diamonds in the first circle might mean that you will make a fantastic killing through your personality by having a relationship with somebody who is very well off. It's a friendly card and prestige card, not as dynamic as the King of Diamonds, but a very good luck-card.

The Ten of Diamonds is money no matter where it hits. It has to do with tremendous and immediate gains and popularity. Large instant rewards, like winning the sweepstakes, as opposed to the other money card, which means a steady, comfortable flow. The Ten of Diamonds is a fantastic amount of money. A killing. Of course, anywhere that you want it to hit is where you place it, and it's lucky in any circle. If you put it up in the ninth, it could be that you will receive money not only from long-distance travel or from philosophical thought, but possibly from publications, radio and television, as well.

Nine of Diamonds is business profit, and it deals with protected business interests, so if you are in stocks and bonds, and you want to insure that there's a nice steady climb, you put the Nine of Diamonds in the second circle or in the eighth. It's a good card for money, not as dynamic as the Ten of Diamonds but it's valuable in secure holdings.

The Eight of Diamonds helps your savings grow. If you're on salary and you start to save at a regular rate, the Eight of Diamonds will cover that area. It's nice, steady, slow and secure, and it's the ten bucks a week type, not the big money; but it's awfully good if you're beginning in life, and you want to force yourself to start saving in a way that's not painful to you.

Eight of Diamonds is a good way to begin anything; put that in your second circle, It also helps if you want to take a vacation and you need to get together enough money for two weeks off; then you put the Eight of Diamonds up in the ninth, and that insures nice, easy money for a vacation, although nothing fantastic. If you're the dramatic type, stick to the nines and the tens for big money.

Seven of Diamonds is your business or marriage partner's luck in money. It's the other person's financial gain. If you put the Seven of Diamonds in the eleventh circle, it means you'll have friends who are doing well. You don't want them to be doing too well, so you just put the Seven of Diamonds up there. But it's their money; it's nothing that comes to you. It has to do with the other person.

Six of Diamonds might be a little money loss because of something like a misplaced receipt or an insurance claim that you didn't collect. It's not so hot, although not as bad as the Six of Spades or Six of Clubs. You are better off keeping the Six of Diamonds out of your spell cast, and if it should fall by itself into your readings, you might recognize it as a slight obstacle in finances.

Five of Diamonds is a destiny card, and wherever it falls it shows that destiny is going to be an important factor in the situation. There is a certain amount of control that we have over all our actions, but occasionally there's one tiny, little slip-up. The Five of Diamonds indicates that something beyond your control has come into the picture, a course of destiny. It could be good or bad. Usually the Five of Diamonds will indicate support from destiny. You may think everything's adding up to a certain conclusion, then the Five of Diamonds pops up into the picture, and something happens that enables you to go even further than you anticipated. Also, if the Five of Diamonds falls in the seventh circle, it might indicate your partner is a little bit immature; possibly, if you're an older man, you have a partner who is a young and giddy female, and if you're an older woman, you've got a guy you might like to keep for a while. It's a peculiar, very tricky card, too unpredictable to use for spell casts.

Four of Diamonds would signify idealism and wisdom, and it indicates wherever you put it, yes, that's going to happen. If you want to make something really take place, put the Four of Diamonds in it. It's a guarantee card, like insurance. It's not powerful to use in spell casts, but it's a nice boost.

Three of Diamonds indicates no. If you're dealing in savings and you want to know, "Should I make an investment?" and if the Three of Diamonds falls in your second circle, that means you should not make that investment. If you're planning a marriage and the Three of Diamonds falls in the seventh circle,

# The Card Spell—The Biggest Spell of All

you might want to think a while before you go through with it. It means stop a minute and think. If you have a husband who's involved with someone else in a passionate affair, you could stick the Three of Diamonds in his fifth circle so that it stops him for a while; he goes over his previous reasons, and it might straighten him out, or he might decide to leave you anyway. It makes him think.

The Two of Diamonds is another wild card. It breaks patterns. If you want to break up a situation, if you want to change, to get out of a direction you're going in—say you've cast a spell and you're not happy with what you've decided to do—put the Two of Diamonds in the particular circle to break it up. Then everything can fall back into place, or you can redesign it or do whatever you want. It's to blast the old in order to create the new. You can put this card in any circle of your card spell and break up existing patterns. Say, for instance, you are living in an area where there is no connection with the city sewer system, and you want everybody in the neighborhood to sign a petition to connect with the city system. Put the Two of Diamonds in the third circle, and you'd get everybody at least agitated in a new direction. There's no end to what you can do with the Two of Diamonds. Don't fool around with it, though, unless it's very important to you that things be shaken up.

Many people are afraid of the Ace of Spades, because they think that it means death—immediate death. I think they overdid this in the opera; it's been very bad public relations for the Ace of Spades from the start. What the card really indicates is a triumph over obstacles. So it might be associated with bad things, because sometimes you must go through terrible things to triumph, and this is a card that indicates that you have survived. It would indicate that something ghastly probably will take place, but you will come through or there'd be no reason for it to show up in a reading. In that one respect it's probably a lousy card, but inasmuch as you pull through, I wouldn't worry about it too much. It's a triumph over very severe obstacles. It doesn't mean death, but it could: The very severe obstacle that you triumph over could be your life, and your triumph over it would be to die and find peace. If you have a chronic, malignant disease and are suffering terribly, and if you were to get the ace of spades, your triumph over that obstacle might be passing on, but that could be interpreted as survival, too. Death is only an isolated interpretation. It really is a very tricky card. If it's placed in the fifth circle, for example, its interpretation is a very tricky affair, a thing that is extremely complicated, one that would have wide repercussions if something happened to bring it out into the open, in the area of a scandal. It indicates a sort of "cloak and dagger" existence and, if you're working for the government, for example, it might be that someone is spying on you, that the whole place is bugged—beware. If it's in the twelfth circle, of course, the jig is up: A horrible scandal is about to erupt concerning your personal affairs. But in general it spells out a triumph over evil.

King of Spades is a nice card, but you wouldn't want a King of Spades in your seventh circle, perhaps, because this would indicate a marriage partner who is the plodding type, very steady but not very exciting, a civil-service type. It's just not adventurous enough for romantic interests. However, if it came in the third circle, it might mean an incident like having to call the police in your neighborhood, and the policeman might be a very attractive individual, this might lead to something. But as a whole it's not all that exciting. There's nothing wrong with wholesome steadiness, but it doesn't turn me on, personally.

Queen of Spades represents your duties in life. It does not mean a dark woman any more than the King of Spades means a dark man. In Diamonds, Hearts and Clubs there is a color application but not so in Spades. If it came in the tenth circle, it might be that the boss's wife is not too happy with your putting the Four of Hearts up there. It would be a disturbance created by somebody who had a duty type of tie on somebody. If it's in your fifth circle, it might be that your lover is married, and can't get out of it. If it comes in your third circle, it's a heavy responsibility. If it's in the first, it might be that an older relative is coming to live with you.

Jack of Spades shows a dissatisfaction in the way things are.

# The Card Spell—The Biggest Spell of All

If it's in your sixth, it's a dissatisfaction with your work; in your fifth, it's a deceitful guy, a dissatisfaction with your lover. If it's in your twelfth, be very cautious, something tricky is indicated in relation to your love affairs. Jack of Spades means a little bit of deceit around you.

There's something lonely about situations where the Ten of Spades is involved. If it should fall in the first circle, you're melancholy; in the second, it's a financial setback; in the third, a poor neighborhood; in the fourth, lonely beginnings; in the fifth, a love affair going on the rocks; in the seventh, it could indicate a divorce or a separation; in the eighth, your partner loses money; in the ninth, a trip being taken because of somebody sick at a distance. It's not a great card to have land anywhere, but if you are casting a spell, and you wish to cause somebody difficulty, you use this card in whatever area is concerned, and there will be unhappiness. It's not violent, but it's not a very happy situation.

Nine of Spades means a responsible attitude needs developing. Say you have it in your second circle; that would mean you have not looked at the entire picture in connection with your finances. In your marriage, the Nine of Spades might mean that you are only looking at today and are not weighing the effect that your actions may have tomorrow in your marriage. It suggests a careful examination of whatever circle it falls into, with a little clearer and more open eyes. If you want wisdom to hit your partner, place this card in the seventh circle. If there is conniving and suspicion at the place where you work, and if you don't want to be put in the position of being a stool pigeon, you could put the Nine of Spades up in the tenth circle, so your boss would come to understand what is going on and straighten things out.

Eight of Spades is an important card. Wherever you put the Eight of Spades it will make the other thing you have going there happen ten times greater. It is a reinforcement of energy. It's a good magical card. Place it on top of any other card you have set out in casting a spell, and it will happen with security and sureness. If the card should fall into a certain circle on its own, it would mean that a thing is going to happen much more strongly than you anticipated, which could be bad or good.

Seven of Spades indicates very strong character, forcefulness, and it could also indicate that a particular situation might be a little touchy at the moment, but the thing is going to improve—later, not today.

Six of Spades shows a depletion of energy in whatever circle it is placed. It means that there will be a lessening of intensity around that particular situation, sort of the opposite of the eight. But the lack of energy, if you see it in a reading, might be a good warning sign to cast a spell and get some energy moving in the right direction for you.

Five of Spades is tremendous, heavy responsibility, and a lot of work, but ultimate achievement. Also, it can indicate that a member of the opposite sex is not too friendly toward you, or if it falls in the sixth circle, it might mean that unsuspected person at work is against you. If it falls in the seventh, it might mean that one of your husband's buddies is setting him against you, or that one of your wife's girlfriends is talking against you. A member of the opposite sex is having a subtle effect on whatever the circle indicates.

Four of Spades signifies little annoyances, and if you find that the Four of Spades falls into a particular circle of your life, then you should be prepared to ignore a lot of what will be happening, because there will be petty annoyances. It doesn't mean that the situation itself is bad, but that you're about to go through some period of aggravation in connection with that circle.

Three of Spades equals tremendous work, responsibility and not too much reward. However, it can indicate insight and wisdom, much as the nine does, provided it comes next to one of the Queen cards. Say that it falls in your sixth circle, which means that your working conditions are absolutely horrible, but in the seventh circle there is a Queen card. That would mean that a woman fitting the description of that card would help solve the problems.

## The Card Spell—The Biggest Spell of All

Two of Spades, again a wild card, is linked with destiny, abrupt changes in direction, and definite, swift triumph.

Ace of Clubs is a powerful card, and it has to do with the human struggle beyond your working conditions, your health conditions, your loves. It has to do with your place in society, and even your place in history, perhaps. It's really a philosophical card, so, wherever it may fall in a reading would indicate that the circle is more important than it appears. There would be more than a love affair, dedication rather than just work, and prestige would be recognition long after death; it indicates a greater sphere of reference than the ordinary run of the mill situation. It also can stand for tremendous emotional strength in whatever activity is involved. If you put it in your seventh circle, it's pretty lucky because that indicates that your marriage partner will be the potent and magnificent type.

King of Clubs. The Kings are the older men, while Jacks represent the younger men in your life, Money and emotion are interwoven in any situation involving the King of Clubs. Strength, knowledge and experience also are represented, so if you put it in the fifth circle, you want an experienced, older lover. If it's in the tenth, your boss is very well-known in the community; if it's in the first, then you yourself, even if a woman, would have capabilities comparable to an experienced male. You have to be very creative in your interpretation of this card. The Kings, Queens, and Jacks, we must remember, are not only representative of people . . . but also of a particular type of experience or characteristic, so that you can use it to interpret what your loved one would look like or what certain people in your life are like. But you should also weigh its other meaning. So the King and Queen of Clubs are indicative of a very moral situation, call it the establishment. The King of Clubs in your fifth circle doesn't necessarily mean that your man is very moral, but it would mean that his relationship with you, even if you never married, would have all the earmarks of a marriage. If you had a love affair with someone indicated by the King of Clubs in the fifth circle, a marriage contract wouldn't matter very much;

you'd be so married you'd probably even file joint income tax returns and would act married to the whole world—a very bourgeois relationship.

The Queen of Clubs also would indicate the link you have between your childhood and adulthood, whatever tie you have to the past, possibly responsibility from the past. For example, if you place the Queen in the third circle, it could mean an old aunt coming to live with you, or you may be supporting someone in the hospital. If it's in the second, you're the one who takes care of your parents. If you're a man and you have the Queen of Clubs in the seventh circle, it's likely that you have a frigid wife; if you're a woman and you have the same card in the same circle, it could mean your husband's mother is coming to live with you. If you want to get rid of your mother-in-law, stick her in the twelfth circle; that puts her in a rest home because the twelfth has to do with institutions as well as secrets, scandals and so forth. Or you might introduce her to your boss by putting her in the tenth. Use your imagination. The Queen may also, if it falls in your first circle, indicate a struggle between what you want to do and what you think you should do. It's a card that calls for care.

Jack of Clubs means an aggressive go-getter type. In the fifth circle it could mean a love affair initiated and sustained.

Ten of Clubs means that you can get pretty much what you want out of whatever situation it's placed into, but it's kind of a cold card. If you fool around with it by putting it in the fifth circle, it may spoil it for you, too. The idea is: You may be able to carry on a love affair and get everything out of it you want, except then it would no longer be a love affair, would it? Put the Ten of Clubs in the second circle, or the tenth or even in the sixth —tenth for your reputation and prestige, second circle for money, and sixth circle for house-work conditions. Don't put it in the seventh, because when you are able to control your marriage so that YOU are getting everything out of it, then you're missing part of real marriage. You're not really involved in marriage if it's all going to be one way; it's too calculated. Use it where it deserves to be used, in business relationships and the like; keep it away from your emotional life. But it does get you anything you want, and if you're a callous type, go ahead, put it in the fifth circle, but don't count on being too happy about the results.

Nine of Clubs brings you a tremendous amount of prestige that rubs off onto you from someone else, so that you are dealing with friends who are well-known, statesmen, government officials, or famous people, at least on the fringe of high society. Placed in the fourth circle it might mean you have a relative who is very rich and very famous and you get nothing concrete out of it; it's like having a very wealthy uncle who's got ten kids. You might as well give up hope.

Eight of Clubs—wherever this goes, you're going to be extravagant with money. It could mean losing money, too, and if it should fall in your fifth circle, it's also connected with an extravagant attitude. If it should fall in the twelfth circle, your flamboyant way of living might get you into money or other difficulty, while the fifth circle means you're a spendthrift with your feelings toward other people. It's a warning card, urging you to be a little bit cautious in whatever area the symbol may fall. It's not too important a card for spellcasting, because you don't want to cultivate that kind of an attitude.

Seven of Clubs heralds arguments and personal weaknesses that might need to be corrected. The card in the fifth circle might mean you are constantly involved in love affairs, and if it's in the seventh, you and your partner have arguments all the time. Your whole way of living may need to be amended. It's a belligerent attitude, and when it affects emotional circles, it's time to shape up. And it's not very good in your money and career circles, either; you need to watch what you're doing wherever this card hits.

Six of Clubs represents wasted energy, energy losses. It's a fighting card, like the Seven and the Five in this suit, but while the Seven has to do with your emotional reaction, the Six relates to how you are affected physically. In the first circle it might mean high blood-pressure or low blood-pressure, some physical reaction to a poor attitude.

Five of Clubs means give it up. If the Five of Clubs falls into a particular circle, it means move on to something else and forget it. It's a lost cause; the thing is over, whatever it is. If it's in the seventh, it means there's no hope, because even if you do avoid the divorce it's going to be a lousy relationship. It's the end.

Four of Clubs, wherever it falls, suggests that you're blinded by a situation. You deceive yourself in connection with whatever life circle the Four of Clubs hits. It's a warning sign to examine your situation; it means you're being dopey.

Three of Clubs means that you are the one who is creating a problem by your actions, no matter how sweet and nice and understanding you think you're being. In your seventh circle, for example, you are the one to blame for marital disharmony, and you'd better investigate, take a look at what's really happening. In the first it means that you have a shortcoming that you refuse to recognize, which is creating some difficulty. In the ninth circle it means that you are a phony, plain and simple; you are philosophically inadequate and refuse to face facts. It's time to think, time to make amends.

Two of Clubs indicates tremendous power in whatever circle it falls. There will be a fantastic intensity of emotion in connection with any circle where this card is placed. Fate triggers sky-high explosions of luck.

Speaking of wild cards, there is one really wild spell that can benefit any life. Put all the Aces and all the Deuces, selectively, in the twelve circles; then support them by some of your appropriate royalty cards, choosing the ones you want. Throw in an Eight, and it'll be like a match in a powder keg; you'll just have a big blast of fantastic events. Ideal for the dynamic amid the dull. It's a terrific spell, and it works very dramatically.

You'll need a tremendous amount of energy before you cast this serious card spell, so I would advise that you get a good sleep and are well-rested. Eat well and get ready for all the fantastic things that will take place, because all hell can break loose. It's awfully good to shake things up and set yourself off in new directions. When you really want to change everything

# The Card Spell—The Biggest Spell of All

that exists, cast a spell of this type, but you have to be very adventuresome to try it.

If you just want to toy with it, that's all right, too, but the results will reflect your attitude. You can make a very big thing of it, though, right from the first step, when you decide just what you want out of life. It is surprising how many people have never taken a moment to figure that out, yet they wonder why they are not satisfied. The meanings and symbolism of the cards can be a little complex, as we said at the start, and many of the cards would never be used in casting spells for yourself, unless to damage, interfere with, or just cloud somebody else's life circles. But for reading the future and warning of upcoming dangers, all cards are important.

The idea of the spell is to concentrate on yourself, of course, but by one additional step described below, the spells, and the readings, too, can be applied to anyone else in your life. There also are things you can do with multiple cards to charge up your spells, and, for those who only want a superficial insight, a handy, one-line, card-by-card general reference is provided at the end of this chapter. The deeper meanings are better, however, and vastly more effective.

First learn to control yourself and your own spells before you begin working with other people. How can you immediately cast a spell for a husband or against a friend, until you know how to do them for yourself. But if you do advance to that stage, remember, in casting a spell for your husband or your marriage partner, male or female, or your business partner, the seventh circle indicates that individual in reference to you. Therefore, the seventh circle would be considered their first circle, and you would set the spell up so that you count out all circles counter-clockwise from that seventh section circle, which has become number one. Same for your brother or sister. For your cousin or your uncle, the third circle becomes the first, so if you were dealing in something connected with this marriage, you would take the seventh circle from the third. If you want to do away with your boss's wife, take the seventh circle from the tenth. Suppose you feel you want to do something in connection with your lover's boss; your lover's boss is the tenth circle from your fifth circle. Your fifth circle is your lover; that's your lover's number one circle, and your sixth circle is your lover's number two circle and so on around. Get it? It is not too easy, so study it a while, and learn the spell for YOU first. For complete control of yourself, in the beginning it helps to draw the pattern as suggested when you lay out the cards; copy it, and carry it with you when you cast a spell. Say you have placed the Ten of Hearts in the first house. Draw it on a piece of paper and carry it with you at all times and set it out on the table in order to gain strength from it, whenever you can do so covertly.

Regarding the absence of a young female figure in the cards, as countered by the Jacks, it should be noted that a *woman* is considered a *woman,* ageless, represented by the Queen. Giddiness is represented by the Five of Hearts, instead, or the Five of Diamonds for youth. A woman can be a woman when she is 16, if she is a woman in approach, while a male finds it very difficult to be a full-blown male at 20; he doesn't have the reputation, character or accomplishment. But a woman can be completely womanly in her teens, and many competent witches are teenage girls. So the five represents immaturity in women; the Queens are all women, any women, any age.

To liven up any spell and provide a kind of insurance backing for its effectiveness, you can—if you haven't already dealt all the cards into the life circles themselves—support your desires with multiple-card placements—alongside, but not inside, the life circles involved. Here are the details on the significance of the various multiple cards; but you never use all of them, and only use the Aces to the Sevens, plus Deuces, of course.

Four Aces together make a tremendous break in the life pattern as far as business and money are concerned. Three Aces together will make a fun situation occur. Two Aces, of the appropriate suits, put together at the proper circle, are good if you've got a plot to create a little bit of havoc in somebody's life.

Four Kings together in the proper circle will bring great honor, prizes, distinction. Use three Kings, if there is a prelimi-

## The Card Spell—The Biggest Spell of All 75

nary business meeting coming up, and you want to get it off on the right foot. Two Kings help unite any people involved in a project, in a brotherly way.

If you're having a party and you put four Queens in the fifth circle, you can be sure it will be a successful party. Three Queens in the twelfth circle would greatly increase the scandal and gossip. Two Queens in the tenth would gain support from the people in your working environment.

Four Jacks—well, that's a handy hand for a homosexual interested in increasing interest from males. Three Jacks has to do with false friends; if you are wondering about a business partner or mate, put the three Jacks in the proper circle and you'll immediately get information from the partner's own false friends.

Four Tens will insure great success in a project, whatever you are doing. If you want to have an affair, put three Tens in the fifth section of your spellcast, that is, if you don't care who it's with and just want an affair quickly. Two Tens are useful if you want to change things, your profession, the attitude of people about you, or if you wish to correct anything; put the pair of Tens beside the proper section.

If you want to be invited to a political dinner, for example, and be favored by the powers that be, put four Nines up in the eleventh circle. Three Nines mean great joy and uplifting of spirit. If you've been tired or sluggish put the three Nines up in the sixth circle, and it's like taking vitamin B—immediately you'll be pepped up. If you've got an enemy with whom you work, put a pair of Nines up at the tenth circle, and they will bug him; he will just be restless and not know what's bothering him.

If you want to take a trip, put four Eights up in the ninth circle. If you want flirtations, put three of them in the seventh circle, or, if you want to dream about love, put two in the twelfth circle.

Four Sevens has to do with intrigues and very low class people, a mixture you'd want to use in connection with somebody else. Three Sevens has to do with older people. If you want to help your grandmother feel better, put them in the third circle. Two Sevens has to do with a great deal of balance and control over anything that you're involved with.

Once more, here is a capsule list of card meanings for quick reference:

Ace of Clubs: money, good news, business.
King of Clubs: an easy-going sort of a fellow.
Queen of Clubs: a sympathetic female.
Jack of Clubs: an alert man, a go-getter.
Ten of Clubs: successful ventures, business or otherwise.
Nine of Clubs: a surprise twist to whatever is going on.
Eight of Clubs: loyal support from people around you.
Seven of Clubs: what is due you in life.
Ace of Hearts: the love card; brings better social life, too.
King of Hearts: male, easy going.
Queen of Hearts: stimulates love situations.
Jack of Hearts: a bachelor
Ten of Hearts: complete fulfillment in a situation.
Nine of Hearts: spiritual joy in your life.
Eight of Hearts: friendly reactions from younger people.
Seven of Hearts: adds calm or serenity to your surroundings.
Ace of Diamonds: startling messages to arrive.
King of Diamonds: a tricky fellow.
Queen of Diamonds: the "other woman" or tricky type.
Jack of Diamonds: a young man, not too trustworthy.
Ten of Diamonds: change of residence.
Nine of Diamonds: an annoyance with material interests.
Eight of Diamonds: sparkly, stimulating events.
Seven of Diamonds: scandals.
Ace of Spades: greatly satisfying conquests.
King of Spades: your enemy, even if he's a blond.
Queen of Spades: a divorcee or widow.
Jack of Spades: a plotting male, up to no good.
Ten of Spades: triggers sadness and melancholy.
Nine of Spades: interfering relative outside immediate family.

Eight of spades: illness triggered by emotional problems.
Seven of spades: all sorts of tricky things, intrigues.
The six, five, four, three and deuce of each suit are all wild destiny cards.

# 5

# How to Concoct a New You—At Home in Your Spare Time

> *"We are the music-makers, and we are the dreamers of dreams..."*
> Arthur William Edgar O'Shaughnessy

Everything that begins in your life should begin nicely clean and brand new to give you confidence that nothing is hanging on from old mistakes to drag you down. To start a new way of operating your life, to completely change yourself into what you want to be, you should start as though with a blank sheet of paper.

You will have to make an inventory of yourself and your life—everything you've accomplished, everything you own. You are what you own; you are what you have done. You must accept yourself on those terms. What you are today is a result of the things you have done or abstained from doing, which is sometimes more of an influence. As you take stock of yourself in following the "New You" blueprint, do not blame others for anything about yourself or your life that you do not like. It may sound tough, but you have to take all the blame yourself.

Every human being on earth has something about him that is unique; we all have something to offer the world that nobody else can offer, even if it's only a dimple. But because we are unique, only we ourselves can decide what we will do, and only we can figure out that list of personal aims called desire. First, you have to stop kidding yourself. How are you ever going to get happiness if you are not honest about what you really want?

What you want and the way you go about getting it is part of the uniqueness about you, and that holds true whether we're talking abut a special sex technique that thrills you or a safe deposit vault full of diamonds. You are going to have to sum yourself up, take your own inventory of dreams and reality, and witchcraft insight will show you how. It is a very different plan from anything you have ever heard before, and, unlike most plans of self-improvement, it works. It works because it's honest. It stands up and faces reality.

For example, everybody has heard wise psychologists advise, "Relax—be yourself." That's the surest route to nowhere ever advocated. Don't relax! Do just the opposite, get yourself all keyed up. The keyed-up, emotionally turned-on you is the best you that the world will ever see. Relax? What for? Too many people are so relaxed they never accomplish what they want. They spend their lives wandering around in the psychological equivalent of hair curlers. Ugly!

Don't be afraid that you can't change. Not everybody can go out and change the world or influence their own environment just by wishing to, but you can certainly change your personal life. And perhaps when your life does change, you will have been an influence on your environment, because what you do will set forth chain reactions that affect everyone around you. It won't be your psychic energy alone that did it. You will be doing something concrete to make the other things happen. Witchcraft of this type is bound to improve what you are, and will also increase your confidence.

The thing to do is this: Write down one thing you want to accomplish. Read it every morning and every night, carry it around. You'll reach the point where you don't even have to look at the words. But you know that piece of paper is in your purse or your pocket and it's happening; eventually it slants everything you do toward the goal. You will make the right moves at the right time and never falter.

Accidents are rare, and practically every disaster that's ever occurred in your life, other than perhaps, getting hit by a tornado, might have been avoided. Almost anything could have been changed slightly, if way back in time you'd made the right move. One subtle difference along the way, and your whole destiny can be altered.

So many people create horrible relationships with the world, and yet they wonder, "How can this happen? I've been so good, I do all I can, yet this is what I get back." They get back exactly what they asked for, unconsciously. Somewhere along the line they developed a pattern of allowing certain things to take place, very minor things perhaps, that eventually built up to a big personal disaster. The thing to do is to correct that tendency from the start, so that if you're not successful next week, you're going to be successful by the end of six months or two years.

You must watch the whole picture and bide your time. There is power in not being rushed, which is not the same as being relaxed. If you are rushed, sometimes you can slip and be overwhelmed by the heat of your own desire. If you play it cool and wait, keyed up and ready, everything is going to fall into your lap.

The approach of writing down and establishing clear desires, then repeating things and carrying the same idea with you, gives you a direct course of action that you may not have had before. It eventually allows you to instinctively discard all the superficial things that are taking place; the unnecessary baggage is dropped and you move at a faster rate.

Your subconscious has taken in information from the time you first feel any sensation at all, and it is full of information as to how to operate. Your conscious mind probably has been distorted and trained by circumstances and people around you. The inner you knows everything. The average man or woman has a fantastic amount of information poured into him constantly every day, and it's there to be tapped. Witchcraft lets

## How to Concoct A New You 81

your subconscious figure out what's right for you in any situation. You may be consciously confused or distracted, but, like a computer, you have stored all the necessary facts to win what you desire. The little objects and chants help your conscious let go and not hold on so tightly to the reins.

Recognize that your conscious mind is a product of environment; your conscious mind has been conditioned by father, mother, husband, children, the entire world. But everything you've read, everything you've seen, even strange and unconnected events have conditioned your subconscious mind. So it's brilliant compared to the outer self. Let it go free!

If you do, you should be able to reach the point where you're able to generate energy by subconscious mental process rather than hard concentration. With control, you should be able to turn on energy. Have you ever talked to someone on the phone who has the flu? They usually answer the phone with a dragging voice. Now that's not necessary, because it's not going to make them feel any better. You should never even pick up the phone without being turned on. Never do anything without turning on. Turning on isn't going to make you die any sooner. In fact, it sustains life. All of these little things can add up to failure. The limp voice on the telephone. Shuffling across the floor with slippers flapping—that's just not necessary. You can walk just as quickly and firmly when you've got a fever. Too often people deliberately fail. They tend to do all they can to break their spirit, subdue their energy. It's this same energy you want and need to get you things. You've got to generate energy in order to get things going. You can take vitamins for the rest of your life, but unless your mental attitude is energetic, you're not going to get what you want. You've got to turn on.

There is no bible of witchcraft, and although there are many books on the market about the history of witchcraft and a few mysterious little things to do, the books are not truly dealing with witchcraft unless it is made clear that mental attitude is the driving force. Anything else is fake, and it's absolutely not witchcraft. So don't waste your time kissing frogs: They won't turn into Prince Charming. The real magic—helped by spells, chants and whatever—must come from within you. That's power enough. It can turn brain tissue into gold, positive gold! Today, in spite of vast knowledge about what makes man tick and what makes man click, many people still want to think that something or somebody else is in control when it comes to their own life. They don't want to accept responsibility for the control of their own lives, their own miseries and disasters. They like to cry, "Somebody else did this." Or, "I would have been different, but my father was mean to me." So long as you persist in this attitude, you are never going to be different or achieve anything. Accept responsibility for everything you do and say. Don't lean on your environment and your inherited characteristics so heavily.

A witch can't poison her enemy's apple, and when he dies, shrug it off with, "It must have been something he ate." A witch who casts a seduction spell can't cry, "Rape." Some people prefer not to be in the driver's seat, because they may never get anywhere or achieve too much. If you want to achieve success, to hit great heights and fulfill all your desires, you've got to risk going down very low, with great despair, because once you recognize that *you've* done it, nobody else, it can hit you very hard. If you can face that, with the help of witchcraft, then the whole world is yours. That's the decisive line. You accept complete control. It's a very heavy burden, but the rewards are fantastic, because all the gains are yours, too. Look around you at successful and unsuccessful people, the happy and the unhappy. One group expresses the thought that things could have been different, but. . . . The majority of people are very content to associate every bad thing that happens to them with an act of another individual or power. If they'd only realize what could be done with limited ability, provided one takes over completely! There is not now and never has been any definitive textbook that all witches follow, yet real witches all do the same things. Real witches do the same things that real people do. Witchcraft just can't really be practiced without the attitude of full control. Read again the spells that include chants that say, "I am the power," or, "I am the cosmos, I am the wind."

From that point, we can move on. Remember what you want to do and what kind of props you will need for spells in order to sustain your faith in yourself. Make an outline, much as people make up a budget. Write out what you want to achieve in life, not specifically now, because it isn't a red hat or an alligator bag, it's the *essence* of the kind of a life that will enable you to have the specific things. Put down, too, what reactions you want from life. If you want energy, you can't just set up a program by which you receive free 100 vitamin capsules every day. Instead, you set up the things that will give you energy. A loose circle, a wide frame, should be placed around your picture of happiness.

Say, for instance, that a person is bored, lonely and not rich. First of all he must give up all his old reasons for being this way. He must stop dwelling on what has created that condition, because that just adds power to the old condition. Then he must start creating an image of the way he wants to live and what he wants to happen. He must visualize this and picture it constantly. Most people do this by occasional daydreams, but it isn't sustained. In order to sustain it while you're occupied doing other things, put it down in a form that you can associate with your desire. Make it concrete; put it in words. Just state the facts as briefly as possible. If you write it out in great detail, it is going to be too tedious, too difficult for you to keep concentrating on the whole thing. So state very clearly and in a few words: One, *this* is what I want, and two, *this* is what I want. Keep it in your desk drawer, and read it regularly. Memorize it. Say it over and over. Keep the list in your purse, and every time you open your purse you will be reminded of it. Put it under your pillow, pull it out, and look at it. At all times fortify yourself with it, keeping it in the forefront of your mind.

Sit in a darkened room, with a candle lit, perhaps incense burning, and some music that you like—all the things that turn you on. When these things are going for you, creating this new experience, tell yourself, "Because every night at midnight I light this candle, I am going to get what I want, everything I want." You don't have to know anything, just be yourself.

Because you light a candle, what you want on your list is going to come to you; tell yourself that aloud, repeatedly. Light a candle: You can trust that because it is something outside of yourself, and it is easier to have confidence in things that are concrete. If you repeat the process regularly, you will advance to the point where a lighted match in a restaurant will reinforce you with all the power of the candlelight ceremony in your home. And pretty soon just visualizing the tiny tip of the candle flame in your mind will have you feeling that you are on the road to success.

Everybody has heard of single-minded people, strong-minded people, the one-track mind type, the kind of driving mentality that gets what it wants. This is the same kind of person you are teaching yourself to be. But this isn't something that happens overnight.

You have to give yourself at least the same length of time you'd give a particular facial cream before you can expect to see results. If you go on a diet, you can't expect results overnight, and witchcraft is something that's going to change your entire life, not just your weight. Crash diets seldom work and neither will crash witchcraft.

Another thing you've got to do is work over years and years of doing things the wrong way, if that's the way you used to do them. It's not necessary to spend the same number of years to start life anew, but it may take you at least a month or six weeks to change your pattern of doing things. But if you follow this practice every day, you will be completely transformed. Within a month you will see the first signs of something new happening.

Knowing that you have the knowledge within yourself to achieve any desire, and that by lighting the candle you'll trigger that knowledge, the more you can relax about it the more quickly you'll trigger that knowledge, the more quickly you'll move toward your goal. These methods have proven very successful for witches in the past. If it is not difficult, it's a good idea to rhyme your major desire. Rhymes are used because there is an hypnotic effect to reading poetry. It flows; you get into the swing of it, and it's easy to remember. You want things to be smooth and flowing. You could either rhyme your own or find a piece of poetry that pleases you and adopt it, substituting your key desire words. You should use the same rhyme over and over, writing it down: "I'm going to have a handsome son, a home and man when next year's done." This will have a subtle effect on your subconscious, so that you will begin to act in the way needed to set into motion events that will result in your obtaining your desires. The primary thing about happiness is that you can't kid yourself: If you do not know what you want, you will never get it.

A man called me on two-way radio recently to ask my advice about an upcoming business deal that he said was very important to him. I felt that his main problem was emotional, not business, so I said to him: "I don't think this business deal is your problem at all. I think you have a very deep emotional problem that is pressing on you right now, and that is worrying you a lot more than this business deal." He admitted it. People always want to discuss their emotional problems, it seems, but find it hard to begin, or perhaps don't know how. One woman who called me during a radio show indicated she was primarily interested in her upcoming wedding. From all the surface facts it would seem that she was extremely happy, a lucky bride-to-be who was about to start out on a happy new life. But suddenly I said to her, "You're not in love with this man at all, are you?" I detected that although she seemed preoccupied with getting married, the partner was a secondary consideration. The girl confessed that she did not love him but could not tell me why she was marrying him. It wasn't for wealth, position or pregnancy, and I can't imagine why she was going ahead with it at all. Just because he asked her?

To know what you want, you have to learn to know yourself. Always study yourself and discover why you do things. Analyze everything. You say, "I did that because I wanted this to happen," always looking at yourself and the things you do and why you do them.

With my own intuition, psychic insight, and a few other things, I try to get people who call me on the two-way radio to look at themselves. They ask me for advice, or they ask me what to do, but I never give advice. I tell them that they are failing to explore their real needs. I say, "What you are really telling me is that you want to do this because you feel..." They say, "Yes." They end up being very happy that someone clarified their thinking for them. They are people who have usually been living in a pattern of hiding from themselves.

People ask me if one can control or create the future. Yes! What you control is yourself. You can change or adapt to things and situations that will be happening.

One of the biggest problems in approaching a new way of life is that so many people look at the future blankly and either deceive themselves or have to admit that they are not sure what they really want. So if you have been unable to clearly plot your list, perhaps you need an inventory to lead you to the insight of what your future should have to make a happy you.

You must sit down and make a list of everything that applies to yourself, even very simple things, like, "I am five-foot-five, I have black hair, I have brown eyes." Put down every statistical fact that bears on your life, because these are what make you real to yourself, and this is the picture you must see clearly. Write down whatever you have done that is of any significance to what you are and the way you live. Even relatives might affect your life and people you react to.

You must even list all your possessions, a complete assessment of everything connected to you. Write it all out. It should be clearly and briefly stated, line by line, item by item, covering you from top to bottom, everything you consider a contributing element to your physical appearance or mental attitudes.

When you have written all these things out, draw a two-column checklist beside it. Examine each item on the list from the point of, "What, of all these things, do I consider important to myself?" The questions for a yes and no in each of the columns are, "What do I like? What is it that bugs me?"

It can't be a matter of what your mother thinks is important, or your teachers or the church or the lady next door. It must be your own secret and personal inventory. Which of these things really matter to you? Do *you* like it or not?

What you possess influences what you are to a great extent, and at this stage you cannot separate or omit any items or relationships from the chart. It all adds up to making you happy or unhappy.

You must be extremely selfish in deciding these desires. Selfishness is often frowned upon as being a poor trait, but it is not. Until you are selfish enough to make a strong individual out of yourself and your desires, you will not be a strong enough person to share yourself with others. Make yourself happy first and then, and only then, will you have happiness to spread around. Those people who sacrifice themselves do it because they get something fabulous out of it. But others will not extend sympathy or hold themselves accountable because you destroy yourself for them. Selfish people, openly selfish ones, are more likeable. You know where you stand. They don't fool around.

In facing the realities that make you what you are, which make your life what it is, you cannot blame an abusive husband or a misguided parent. *You* have contributed to these situations. *You* can remove yourself from them. No sick mother has ever prevented her daughter from marrying for 45 years—unless the daughter wanted to avoid the perils of marriage. No mother has brought you up so badly that your life is ruined. No one mistake, or series of them, can have ruined your life. The mere fact that you are alive, that you can recognize the situation you are in and its need for improvement, makes you a part of what has happened.

This is not to say that because you are displeased with your married life that you must pack up and walk out on your mate and children—although sometimes this is the only answer to a hopeless situation. But sometimes the "old you" walking out and the "new you" walking in will be sufficient. A woman called me once and told me that, after 30 years of marriage, she was going to leave her husband. After 30 years of knowing a human being and reacting to him, she was willing to never see him again. It was as though she had had absolutely no experiences with this individual that in any way were connected with her life. No memories. Even without considering sex or love, if you live next door to a guy for 30 years you establish *some* thing between you. She said she never liked him, she always had trouble with him. Well, an important part of her marriage seemed to be based on the fact that she was living with somebody she didn't like; she liked *that*, and if she left, she would miss hating him every day. Something in the relationship must have satisfied or pleased her in some way, or she wouldn't have stuck it out for 30 years. People do not suffer. The first inclination is to protect ourselves and this we do. When there is suffering we get out; when we linger, it may mean that we like it.

Another woman was planning to leave her husband to start a new life. She told me that she felt nothing for him; that was why she was leaving. She feels nothing because he feels nothing; they live together feeling nothing, and when they split up they will go on feeling nothing: Divorce will not change the situation. She will still feel nothing because she is giving out nothing to react to, but is just waiting for somebody to make her react. Leaving him won't change her, or her life.

Too many people let themselves get caught in a sort of limbo-land, situations that do not demand too much from them and that pay meager dividends of happiness. This "safe" spot may gradually destroy your life or just explode in your face. It is simpler, easier, and far more rewarding to make a commitment, declare what you want and go after it.

There is a tendency to seek out constant situations. But life is dynamic; it changes every day. If a constant situation to you means lack of motion, nothing happening, then you are playing dead. If you play dead, you can end up dead. It's a very tricky thing, because some people go into situations like marriage expecting that the other person is going to give their life meaning. They want to dedicate themselves to this other person, give themselves over to this other person and become part of their life. Such an attraction is doomed, for if an individual has nothing going for himself, the excitement of the alliance is missing from the start, and, if the other person fails to sustain the relationship, then there is no relationship, there is no life.

# How to Concoct A New You

Have you ever heard someone say, "If he leaves me, I'll die."? Baloney! Nobody dies because some other person leaves. The other person doesn't matter; it is you that matters. When you DO die is when you stop doing what you do, what makes you what you are; that's why, if you live through another person only and have no life of your own, their departure is like killing you. But it's suicide, not murder.

Living your life is what you do, and nobody else can really do it for you. People often ask celebrities and famous successes if they have some outlet, a hobby, as a relief from their work, and most often the celebrity is surprised by the question, because his work *is* his life. If he does have a hobby, he pursues it with the same energy and zest as he does his chief occupation. The implication of such a question is that, for example, an actor or actress spends 12 hours a day working in front of cameras only biding their time until they can get home and do what they really want. The fact is, they spend their days being themselves, living their lives, and why would they want to change that when they went home? You never stop being you.

If you are waiting until you get off work to be yourself, you are wasting a major part of your life. If your work does not agree with you then you must change it, not change yourself. If you are waiting for something to happen, something to change before you start doing what you really want to do—later, always later—then you are wasting your life. So much of life is wasted waiting to live, to feel, to be alive, to love—and soon life is over and it is too late.

How many things happen to you when you're in an emotional slump? None. Things happen when you are turned on, active, dynamic. It is there, inside you. And starting to act creates more energy in you, charges you up.

You've got a wonderful mechanism for reacting, and you should enjoy using it, feeling everything you've got, while you've got it. If you wait for the next time around, you're placing an awful big bet on reincarnation.

When people say, "Relax and be yourself," that's not really yourself. Yourself is everything you've learned to do, to think, to cover up and hide. The you is a learned thing, something shaped. When you relax everything you've shaped, then there's no more you.

A witch wants great things to happen in her life, but she never thinks that they are going to be just handed to her. A witch wouldn't want them through another individual. That would be second-hand life. What you want should come to you as a result of your own energies and efforts, from something that comes out of yourself. You can't duplicate that sensation, because when you get something that way, you've done it all yourself. You take full credit.

Everybody has something to offer, the power to get what he wants. There is nothing that can beat what you are. The one thing that everybody else lacks is you, your life. You have that: You are the only one living your life. Every shape, every form has a chance to achieve some sort of joyful existence, and you are no exception.

Look around you; look at people. Appearance is not an important factor. There are fat, ugly people who have handsome mates attracted to them by something else inside them, some energy. It doesn't matter if you're tall, short, fat, skinny or bald; it is what you project, what you are offering that is important, not how you look. Of course, we try to make the best of our physical characteristics, but, bumpy nose, gray hair or whatever, let's face it, none of us are beautiful, at all stages of our lives. But what your personality projects is what you'll get back from the world. There are many pretty people who are extremely unhappy individuals.

On the other hand, there are diets, plastic surgeons, skin specialists, cosmetics and exercises, and other ways to go about being as attractive as possible if that's important to you. Study the people around you. Not the people of films, television and magazines who are superhuman and unreal. The people you must study are those you'll find by going out into the streets, into banks, post offices, anywhere where there are masses of people. Look at them. They are people who are married, or single, well-dressed, or not, well-proportioned, or not. Look at their faces, the way they carry themselves. If you lack confidence, such a study will reap huge benefits, because you'll realize that most of the people in the world are not very much to look at, even though most of them are making it, making steps toward happiness. What's holding you back?

Many people think that witchcraft will give them a quality of being mysterious. What has being mysterious to do with witchcraft? I've known a lot of dull and stupid women who were mysterious. They had no control and were accomplishing nothing. They were a mystery to themselves, and this is what they projected. A witch is neither overly mysterious nor overly open. You can have any kind of personality and practice witchcraft.

It doesn't mean that you should go around your neighborhood broadcasting the fact that you have taken up witchcraft. Maybe it helps when you're trying to quit smoking, to tell everybody that you're quitting cigarettes. If letting people in on the secret that you're practicing witchcraft is liable to put you in the position of being goaded, bugged and kidded by friends who do not believe, then why put yourself in line for this kind of bothersome torment at a time when you're beginning something new? I wouldn't advise you to go out and say you're practicing witchcraft, because most people, with all the old false conceptions of witchcraft, will think you are a nut. Once it's working for you, then go out and tell the world what you've done if you want to. But at the start, if a friend says, "What's come over you lately, you're a completely different person?" your reply should just be a noncommittal, "Oh, am I?" Friends all interject their reactions into something unusual, and most of the time the reactions are not really their own, but something handed down to them. They don't know what they're talking about. In situations like this, it's best to keep quiet until you've got the control you need. Then nobody will laugh. They'll copy you.

People who try to make themselves over completely sometimes get impatient. If you try a spell for six weeks and nothing happens, and if it's something that's new to you, then six weeks is not a terribly long time for you to get into shape, or reshape, as the case may be. It's a day- to-day way of thinking, an approach, a way of life that must be developed, and if it takes longer for some people than others, it does work. Look at it the way you look at anything else you get involved in: Women learn to put on makeup. The first time many come out looking freaky. Women don't learn the best way to do their hair overnight; it takes a while. Learning to make love, and all its variations and subtleties is something also that takes time. So what's the rush with witchcraft?

You are going to be reborn; you've got to make up your mind to it. You must start as an embryo in the world of witchcraft and expand in power from there. But once it happens, you grab hold of a whole new life, a more dynamic and happier one. That's worth working for.

# 6

# Your Lucky Numbers and How To Use Them

*"This is the third time; I hope
Good luck lies in odd numbers;
There is divinity in odd numbers,
Either in nativity, chance, or death ... "*
*William Shakespeare*

When you are dealing with numbers, there is a comfortable and organized system that exists around you. There are numerical values to everything, every form of life. Every piece of energy, every chemical reaction has a mathematical equation to represent it. Even the atomic structure of things is organized in a way that can be represented by numbers. Every element known to man has a numerical value based on its atomic weight or the number of protons and electrons in its individual atoms. Numbers are basic to life; they are inherent in all things. So if we want to establish control over things, as witches do, it is natural that we explore the relation between us and the numbers that mean something to our lives.

We are not ruled by numbers, although sometimes it might seem so. The force of the moon, the astronomical arithmetic by which we count off our months, affects the tides. All our days are numbered by a calendar that is attuned to the motion of the planets and the forces of the universe. A woman in her menstrual cycle counts the days. The blood that flows in our veins resembles the structure of the salt water that flows in oceans, oceans governed by the moon, oceans from which, evolution says, we ourselves originated.

Each color we see has its own vibratory number-value. The number of vibrations determines what color registers in the brain.

Sound also reaches us in terms of so many vibrations, so that everything we hear is a reaction to so many pulsations per second. And I'm sure that each person emits a vibratory level that makes other people respond in various ways. There is our heart beat, our pulse, our blood-pressure level, our brain waves, and the basic metabolic rate that determines the pace of our individual consumption of energy—all expressed in numerical values that differ slightly for every person on earth. Numbers belong to us. Numbers are what we are, to a certain extent. People who have seen themselves helplessly reduced to social security numbers, bank account numbers, military service numbers, auto licencse numbers, and many more, often feel that there is a pressure to wipe out the individual and replace him with a numerical value.

Photographs of the moon and Mars were transmitted back to earth in the form of computer numbers, which does not mean that there are a lot of numbers floating around in outer space; but it does mean that anything in life can be assigned a numerical value, such as the computers that were fed information translating photographic levels of light and darkness by the number.

Numbers in themselves are not potent. We give them a potency. This must be understood, and controlled.

Some people live by numbers. They apply the numbers that are significant to their own lives to each day, to everything they do. Gamblers do it. Horse racing enthusiasts come up with whole betting systems geared to mathematical logic.

Several years ago a man came to me from Argentina. He was connected with horse racing and was bringing a string of

## Your Lucky Numbers and How To Use Them 95

horses up to Hollywood Park. He wanted to know what would happen. I agreed to help him. I asked for the exact birthdates of the horses, jockeys, and everyone else involved. Using the birthdate as a jumping off point for a look into the future, one must consider the fact that there is no date in our lives to which we react more than our birthdates. But did it apply to horses? How did I know? I'd never tried it before. It was difficult to get the birthdates of the horses, because all horses are registered as born on January first of whatever the year may be, but they wrote to South America and managed to get them. I made astrological charts for every horse as well as all the people involved, and when my computations were complete I told them which horses were best for which days, which races, and which jockeys. By racing certain horses on certain days with special jockeys, and betting them heavily, they made a real killing. Of course, these men were very strongly motivated for money and winning. I myself only made a small amount of money. It wasn't that I lacked confidence in my forecasts. I'm just not interested in horse racing. I'm hardly conservative, I'm just not the type who goes to the races.

If they hadn't come to me I never would have considered the races a source of fortune, but the reluctance is not because of fear that commercialism might abuse my powers. Many psychics don't believe they should be paid for being telepathic; they feel that it lessens the force. Well, does buying a Rembrandt for two million dollars make it a less valuable painting? I don't believe that a witch can dissipate her powers. I think that the more you do something the better you get. There's a gain of energy, not a loss. So I remain powerful, controlled, brave and unafraid, but perhaps disinterested in betting.

Another time I did charts combining astrology and numerology for two brothers who wanted to make a fortune at the Caliente race track in Mexico. They have a five-ten bet, like the daily double only ten times as big. If you can pick the winners in five or six consecutive races, you can win thousands and thousands of dollars. I worked out a system for them, basing it almost entirely on numbers, including their own personal numbers, the time they would be going to Mexico for this venture and other factors. I picked everything by hours of the day. What I actually was giving them were my calculations of which numbers would be best for which hours of the races. The names of the horses were never a factor; I didn't even know them. It was a matter of choosing, perhaps, the fourth horse in the fifth race for the fifteenth hour of the day. So, they took all this information and set off. Something happened to them on the way down there. A small accident delayed them so that they arrived a day late, and they were panicky because they felt that all the information applied to the day before. Well, they took a deep breath and went ahead and bet the numbers anyway. Fate is fate, they figured. The upshot was, they did not win the grand five—ten prize, but they did win—on the basis of their day-old information—the prize that goes to anyone who picks all but one of the winners. Now that's not bad: It was thousands of dollars, and it meant they bet on the winners in five out of six consecutive races!

    I know how to go about picking such things, by feeling my way into it. Door prizes for instance: I can usually tell somebody the time at which they should buy their ticket in order to win the prize. You can fool around with these things, and I do it for fun, but I'd rather aim for something bigger, more meaningful.

    Lucky numbers are discovered by old, standard systems that vary little from country to country all over the world, even where they have different alphabets; they count them the same way to translate names into numbers. There is also the system that uses your birthdate. Add the number from your birth month to the birth date, and then the number of the birth year. At each point the number is broken down into the smallest possible figure, so that it never equals more than nine. I will explain that in more detail later.

    Translating your name into your lucky number is done with an international formula. Witches go another step and cast a spell in connection with the result:

# Your Lucky Numbers and How To Use Them

```
1 2 3 4 5 6 7 8 9
A B C D E F G H I
J K L M N O P Q R
S T U V W X Y Z
```

Following this system you can see that the values of A, J and S are the same as the number one; B, K and T are number two; C, L and U are number three; D, M and V are number four; E, N, and W are number five; F, O, and X are number six; G, P and Y are number seven; H, Q, and Z are number eight and I and R are number nine. Let's take the name Bob Smith as an example of counting a lucky number from a name.

Bob is represented by the number one.

$$\begin{array}{ccc} B & O & B \\ 2 & 6 & 2 \end{array} = 10 = 1$$

As Bob is a number one name and Smith is a number 6 name,

$$\begin{array}{ccccc} S & M & I & T & H \\ 1 & 4 & 9 & 2 & 8 \end{array} = 24 = 6$$

Bob Smith, one plus six, adds up to a number seven name.

If Bob Smith wants to figure out his pattern for a particular day, there are a few other computations to make. His number seven name refers to his environmental background, his heritage. We look at his birthdate for his destiny number. Say it was January 1, 1930. That is the first month and the first day, which adds up to two, and then 1930 would be computed this way: one and nine are ten and three are thirteen; one and three are four so 1930 is a number four year. Adding the one and one from the birth date and month, we arrive at the figure six representing Bob Smith's birthday. As seven is his name value and six is his birthdate, the total makes him a number 13, which reduces to four (one plus three).

Now that he has established that, he can look at any day, say June 4, 1971, and tell his fortune by numbers. June 4, which is the sixth month, a six, plus the date, four, equals ten; the one and zero equal one, plus the year, which adds up to a nine, digit by digit, so with the original one we are back to ten or one again: it's a number one day. For Bob Smith, whose name and birthdate add up to four, it is a number five day, however. This can be done with every day of your life, and if you know the symbols that relate to the numbers you have a guiding key for every fraction of the future.

According to the ancients, number one is symbolized by the sun, number two by the moon, number three by Jupiter, number four by Saturn, number five by Mercury, number six by Venus, number seven by Uranus, number eight by Mars and number nine by Neptune. One old interpretation equates Pluto to the number zero, but others place a value of twenty-two on Pluto, which is an exception to the rule of reductions. If your birthdate adds up to twenty-two, this number is not converted to a four as the sum of two and two, because twenty-two has a special meaning from antiquity. What are the characteristics related to the various numbers and planetary influences?

Number one, the sun number, stands for responsibility, aggressiveness, pioneer spirit, moving out in front. If it's a day you are referring to, the type of activities you'll be involved in have to do with authority, logic, confidence, power, beginnings of new things, optimism, youth, magnetic forces and strength.

Number two, the moon number, may appear feminine by society's standards, but we are only referring to temper, so a woman could be ruled by number one and still be very much female, and a man could be ruled by number two and be very male. If you were a number one female, for example, you'd be a little more energetic and aggressive than the average female, but that doesn't mean you're not feminine. Number two, however, is the counterpart of that. It's the other side, the sensitive, sympathetic, vulnerable, absorbing self. So while the number one individual is going out toward what he wants, the number two person or situation accepts and absorbs, but it doesn't mean any less strength. Absorbing rather than overpowering can be just another way of getting there. Two is more emotional, while one is more logical.

Number three, the Jupiter number, is neither logical nor emotional. It's spiritual. This is the individual who has a belief, an intuitive grasp of a situation rather than a logical or emotional approach. A number three day would be one in which there's more fun than number one or two. It might be a day to go to a party. A number three person tends to be creative, a diversified personality. There might be a touch of good luck to the day in a way; there's a hand of destiny involved. A number three individual is someone who walks away unhurt from an automobile accident; he's the guy who wins at the races. If you come up with a number three day, by adding up what your environment made you and your destiny number, that's a good day to go to the races and bet all your lucky numbers.

Number four, the Saturn number, has to do with tradition, being conservative, avoiding reckless behavior, employing natural resources and power. It has to do with solid foundations, so if you are a number four type then you tend to be cautious, steady, looking for security, but, of course, your luck can be something else again. In the same way that one spells going out like a rocket, number two leans to absorbing and number three to exuberance, number four is symbolized by caution.

Number five, the Mercury number, and its vibrations, are linked with mental and manual aptitude. It's fast, quick—anything associated with speed. A number five individual could be a comic, but that doesn't mean that everything about number five is funny, because another interpretation could be a series of tragic events. But whatever happens, happens quickly. A number five is a reactor, rising quickly to the occasion, and a number five day might be one in which many things are happening that require your immediate response. It could mean travel, too; a lot of movement.

Number six is the Venus number, which vibrates to emotion. Love, partnership, luxuries, riches and beautiful things are involved. It is the kind of day when you'd get a present from a loved one. If you're a number six type you are probably very extravagant. This type spends a lot of money on clothes, cosmetics and food; it's a sensual number.

Number seven, the Uranus number, has to do with progressive thoughts, inspiration, cycles and patterns. A number seven type would be the kind of person who is orderly to the extent of putting things in categories, labeling them, and compartmentalizing various segments of his life. You might be a career man who lets his wife know nothing about his business, for example, or a married man whose wife hasn't the slightest inkling about his love affairs because you are very careful in the way you operate. A number seven day is probably one in which a person would clean up and organize his life, straighten out past difficulties. Inspirational forces and intuition are also involved with this number.

Number eight, the Mars number, is a primitive number that deals with the physical self. A number eight person is one who inclines toward working more with the body than the mind. It could be a very strong or oversexed woman. Interest in sports, combat, anything associated with physical activity are included in the number eight sphere.

Number nine, the Neptune number, is a detective type, someone who digs in deep, sensitive to things below the surface. A number nine person might be psychic, and a number nine day might be romantic, not in the way of a number six day, (connected with love), nor in the number eight way of physical love, but rather more in a communion-of-spirits way. Number nine days also are those in which you reap the accumulated benefits of a long time—a harvest day. A number nine person might be the end product of centuries of evolution and have insights far beyond those of his fellow man.

Number 22, the Pluto number, as indicated earlier, is a special case. If your first name counts out to 22 for example, don't change it: you would have to add it to four to get the count of your whole name, of course, but you'd have to remember that part of you always vibrates to that 22 force. If your whole destiny number comes out to 22, leave it that way, and if your pattern for the day adds up to 22, don't convert it either. A number 22 person is marked, destined to do something and would sacrifice himself for a goal, an ideal. You feel that the ideal is the thing, and this applies to your love affairs, your work, everything. If a 22 day is coming up, it is an important day; something will happen that day that you'll remember for a long time.

How do you look at all the numbers that apply to you? You have four numbers in all, three of them stationary and one that changes every day. Your name represents your environment, because your parents gave you that name and raised you to be what they considered that name to represent; and you react to the name all your life. So by adding up all the letters in your name, you have the number representing your environmental gift, your inheritance. The month, day and year you were born total your *destiny* number. If you didn't have a name you'd still have a life with that destiny. For your third number, add your inheritance and your destiny numbers, and you've got yourself, facing the world, the total of *your luck* and *your background.* Add that to the present day, and that's how your whole aspect adds up for the 24 hours at hand.

That's the kind of approach that is taken when you go to the races, for example. The whole point is to add your personal numbers and all the numbers involved, so that you've got your name going, your birthdate, the present day—all to be added up to the first race, the second race, and so on, so that you can come up with the horse number and race number most compatible to you and your numbers. Take, for instance, the fourth horse in the fifth race; you have a nine, which, as was indicated, marks the payoff of the accumulation of previous days. Now, if you add that nine to yourself and come up with a three, it might be a windfall type of bet because that indicates an up-type situation. But, and this one point is very important, the interpretation would still be up to you to know if it's a good force for you or not, and you'd have to decide whether to bet, and how much— which is another number, too.

You can examine the numbers for any move, like going on

a trip or vacation, signing a contract, launching a love affair, whatever the occasion. And, you can combine your number with your loved one's to take a look at what kind of relationship you're going to have. This takes a little know-how, but it seems to follow very truthfully, when you let your mind control. For example, any married woman undergoes a change when she marries, and furthermore, she has changed her name.

### ELIZABETH TAYLOR

For an example of how a married woman changes when her numerical representation is altered by marriage, let's examine a well known case, a woman with lots of experience in the field —in marriage, not numerology, that is: Elizabeth Taylor.

Elizabeth is a number seven and Taylor is a number one, so Elizabeth Taylor, girl star, is a number eight, ruled by Mars, an influence that has to do with conquests, victory, determination and strength. This is on top of her first-name proclivity for the Uranus seven, a very exciting, adventuresome, intuitive, high-strung personality, which does describe Elizabeth Taylor.

Then she finds herself married, in succession, to Conrad Hilton, which turns her into a number five as Elizabeth Taylor Hilton, because she isn't an ordinary woman who marries and drops her maiden name. Elizabeth Taylor Wilding also becomes a number five, but when she married Mike Todd she became a number six. When she became Elizabeth Taylor Fisher she turned into a number one, and as Elizabeth Taylor Burton she emerges as a number eight.

Let's take a closer look at the subtle changes in the person, as an actress and as a married woman, as these life situations, and the numbers connected with them, changed through the years.

We break down the first name to a seven. We explain that this is a jazzy personality, and this jazzy personality has to express itself through Taylor, which is a number one name, making her a number eight. We've explained what that is. When she married Hilton, and when she married Wilding, oddly enough, both those names did the same thing to her. Elizabeth

Taylor as a Elizabeth Hilton OR Elizabeth Wilding vibrates to number four. That is a restrictive influence. It may be good for finances and it may be good for building, and you must take into consideration that she had two sons with Wilding; so she benefited from the marriage in one area. However, the Saturn constrictions and controls were not compatible with her nature as a number eight dynamic personality.

However, both Wilding and Hilton caused her to be a number five in her profession. Elizabeth Taylor Hilton and Elizabeth Taylor Wilding are both five. Five is ruled by Mercury, which makes her adaptable, always in the limelight, having a variety of interests. It provides an aura of seeking, constantly groping, trying to find your place. They did turn her on to exploring herself, which may not have occurred with someone else to begin with. They were quite different, the two men. But we are interested in what their personalities did to her, not what they were. Her reactions are important, and to them she reacted with a Saturn influence. No two people are alike and we are not really concerned with how people are: it's how you think they are, and how you *feel* about what you think they are! Whatever their personalities may have been and how opposed their personalities were to each other, her reaction was identical. People look at a marriage and they say, "Oh, you have so much fun; you do this together, and you do that together." In truth someone may be dying inside and miserable in the relationship, who knows it but the person who is suffering? So we don't score each personality, just her reaction to that personality. She divorced both of them, which is the same reaction. So with these two men she was number four, and professionally she was number five. Professionally perhaps it was a period of value to her. She sought in her work what she didn't find in her home, and it pushed her into exploring her own potential and her talents and possibly created many opportunities that would open up later and bear fruit because of the friction at home.

Then she married Todd. She is Elizabeth, number seven, and the name Todd vibrates to a number seven. She is comfortable with that. Together Elizabeth Todd comes to number fourteen, which is five, so as Mrs. Todd she has achieved the personal image that she was playing with when she was Elizabeth Taylor Hilton and Elizabeth Taylor Wilding, the professional actress. She achieved in her marriage with Todd the essence of what up until that time only her career gave her, and this was a satisfaction because now she could get this by just being Elizabeth Todd. She didn't have to be the actress. When she was Elizabeth Taylor Todd she vibrated to a number six. This is a Venus vibration and it has to do with luxuries, attraction, love, warmth and emotionalism, a vibrant situation; so she was able, as Mrs. Todd, to add a dimension to her personality as an actress. We must, before going onto the next step, look at Todd. Todd is number seven, Mike is number two. The number two vibration with the number seven makes a number nine. His personality was a number nine type. People who believe in reincarnation believe that number nine types are the end of a cycle. They are the end of many lives, having been reborn many times. According to numerology, he has an insight that can only be gained through multiple lives. Number nines instinctively react to things as though they'd been around for millions of years. He was a number nine type who would have given support to any personality, would have made any personality feel themselves. He brought her out of herself.

Then came Fisher. Elizabeth's a number seven, Fisher's a number eleven. We put them together to get nine. As Elizabeth Fisher she was able to imitate emotionally what she felt with Mike Todd. As Mrs. Fisher she could keep the essence of Mike Todd around her. Her name is a number nine, which is what Mike Todd was. Fisher was compatible only so long as she needed Mike Todd near her. But by marrying Eddie Fisher she changed herself to Elizabeth Taylor Fisher, and that had a catalytic effect upon her, much the same as Mike Todd was a catalyst who affected everything he touched. She married Fisher, the number nine name, changing herself into Elizabeth Taylor Fisher, number one. And whether she liked it or not, she was thrown into a new cycle, the beginning of a new personality, an independent, aggressive, responsible individual with more

# Your Lucky Numbers and How To Use Them

authority in life. Whether she liked it or not, she was the leader in her marriage. She didn't marry him with that intention. She married him to have the sentimental essence of Todd and was thrown into a new role, completely against her inclinations, to a new cycle. So it couldn't last because she changed. Number nine is a Neptunian number. It's mysterious, and it's spiritual, and it has to do with all the hauntings and ghost-like situations of the world. While she was wallowing in this number nine vibration she was thrown into the number one cycle. It was the beginning of her destiny, a rebirth.

So she was reborn as a number one individual and met Richard Burton. As Elizabeth Burton (Burton vibrates to number nine), she becomes a number seven, which Elizabeth is anyway. It's the Uranus number, so with Burton she is Elizabeth, period. She is not Elizabeth Taylor and she is not even Elizabeth Burton. She is herself for the first time in this particular situation. It feeds her. It allows for growth because she is free. For the first time in her life she is what she is. As a star Elizabeth Taylor Burton vibrates to the number eight. We know to begin with that Elizabeth Taylor vibrated to the number eight, so being Mrs. Burton has allowed her to be Elizabeth Taylor, and if there's anything to numerology at all, she has become herself with this last marriage.

The planetary patterns coincide with particular events. Not necessarily because the planets themselves influence us, but possibly due to mathematical cycles evolving into particular events. For instance, Uranus takes about 84 years to go around the sun, which means we are dealing with a mathematical influence rather than a planetary one—perhaps. There may be an influence that as yet has not been recognized, but the fact that an event takes place in the skies, coinciding with an event on earth, may be part of a mathematical pattern.

Your cycle is not the same as anyone else's, and if you can take the moment of your birth and break it down, say, into hundred day cycles or thousand day cycles, eventually you would see a pattern developing. You could chart your life by digging back into your past and seeing what occurred every hundred days, every thousand days, or every four thousand days, and once you have a picture of what did take place, you can then project into the future and come up with some interesting material. You can't find the meaning of your life printed in a book, but you can learn how to figure it yourself, and from your experience interpret what's about to happen. First, you figure out how many days you have been alive.

Take somebody who's 25 years old: In 25 years you have lived about 9,000 days. In your 25th year you have experienced a short cycle. When you are born you are the center, the sun. Everyone reacts to you for approximately the first two years. The next two years, ages two to four, you are reacting to everybody else, which is the moon cycle. Between four and six years of age is the Jupiter cycle where you start to seek out what is around you. From six to eight, you develop the potential to be molded. Continuing, by the time you hit 25, you are in a Mars cycle, and you have ended a whole role of life and are about to move forward; you're ready to explode into a new level.

You can break this down and enlarge your cycles so that you have roughly 1,000 days for each one. But you could double it and allow 2,000 days for each cycle. The point is that there is no established concept of the number of days per cycle. You could use 10 years per cycle if you were going to live 90 years. You could say 10 years were your sun years, the next 10 to 20 were your moon years, 20 to 30 were the Jupiter years and 30 to 40 would be Saturn years of hard work, control and discipline. From 40 to 50 would appear a restless seeking of something once again, your Mercury cycle. Mathematically you should be able to calculate cycles within cycles, and break it down to your daily, weekly or monthly cycle.

Look at cycles of 10 year cycles. During the first 10, attention is focused on you. In the next 10, you are reacting to everyone else and from 20 to 30 you are involved in the Jupiter cycle; this is creative and may be why this is suddenly the potent time for sex; it's the creative urge. Jupiter has to do with creativity, a joyous response to situations around you. From 30 to 40 is the Saturn cycle, denoting restrictions; 40 to 50, Mercury, making abstract things real. Communication is important at that point; the average individual wants to be very certain that everybody understands him verbally. From 50 to 60 are the Venus years. This is the time when you have accumulations of luxuries and comforts, developed over the past. The 60 to 70 Uranus cycle is the time of being full of information, the time when there are things outside your intimate circle, when you become very important and useful to the community. That's the time when your life takes on meaning other than your own private world. You're universal in your actions. And 70 to 80, the Mars years, have to do with determination, fortitude and power. The Neptunian cycle, from 80 to 90, is more of the dreamy state and also can be a source of inspiration to the people around one; it's a shame so many people of that age are senile, because rather than being inspirational, they usually end up in a home. That's the large cycle during which they could inspire other people.

You could chart yourself by the week, and you could find out what part of the week or month you were vibrating to Mars or Jupiter.

You see, inasmuch as the planets aren't really doing anything to us, they're useful in mapping out life patterns. If you go to a dance where there's continuous music, it doesn't matter at which point you arrive. Your time at that dance begins when you put your foot on the floor and take up the beat. Everybody's got the beat, and you're all dancing.

You can pick up the numerical beat by establishing the day you want to begin charting a cycle. There might be a little bit of confusion until you catch on to your rhythm, but it's smooth sailing after that. Decide your number one day, your sun rule day, and from that point on you can chart your next month of activity. In so doing, you will eventually establish an insight into what your particular rhythm is. You will learn that on a sun day such and such a reaction occurs, and on a moon day you have another reaction. This way you'll have complete control over which days are best for you to begin new projects or to enter a romantic situation. You alone will understand your own cycle. You won't need a fortune teller.

## NEW-LIFE SPELL

Suppose you decide to be reborn on a particular date. Establish it when you wish. You will have to find out when the sun will rise in your particular location by calling the local planetarium or newspaper office. At the moment of sunrise, you must have prepared nine gold colored candles and have a photograph of yourself in order to make yourself more real. Ring the nine golden candles around the photograph. Chant over and over to yourself for about five minutes, "I am in control. I own myself. I will choose what I want to have happen to me." Let the candles flame for about 10 minutes at sunrise, and you will have the number one cycle from that point.

There shouldn't be any one day that you consider in advance a bad day, because every day has its own essence and its own nature. The only thing wrong with anything in life is to use it in a way that is not compatible. There isn't any bad luck day, full of hard luck or mistakes. Don't look at a day and say, "Today is a Saturn day so I'm not going to get out of bed." Instead go out and do everything that should be done on a Saturn day. If it's your sun-day cycle, the number one day, take the initiative in everything. That doesn't mean that you must be afraid to be passive. It means that if you take the initiative on that day you will have great success. Being passive doesn't mean that you'll have a disaster, it just means that you aren't utilizing the day to its fullest potential.

On your number two day, which is the moon day, you will do well by being receptive to other people's ideas. That doesn't mean that you can't go out and assert yourself that day. It means that if you were more receptive you would possibly have accomplished more. The influences just show where you will have your best accomplishment.

Number three, the Jupiter day, indicates you would do well

to spend your time with creative activity. This could include giving a party, having a romance, exploring the many sides of every situation. It's a good day to take an examination, but that doesn't mean you're going to fail if you do it on another day or that it's disastrous not to have your party on the number three day. It's just that if you do have a party on the number three day, it's going to be a better party.

The number four day, a Saturn day, doesn't mean doom and gloom and friction and all horrible things, but if, on a number four day, you decide to establish permanent foundations in a particular direction, you'll succeed. If you decide to build a house on a number four day, it will be a better house. If you decide to break a habit on a number four day, you'll have more luck in breaking the habit. You could quit smoking on a number three day, but you'd have a better chance on a number four day.

The whole object is to use the cycle for what its worth and not to be afraid when you haven't used it. If you have a beautiful crystal glass in your cupboard and don't use it, it doesn't lessen its value or make it useless. But how nice it is to use at the right time, when you have company or just want to be in a good mood.

A number five day, a Mercury day, is a good time to send letters to people that you haven't contacted in quite a while. It's a good day to pay your bills. It's a day when it will be easier for you to sit down and get your checkbook out and pay off the people who should be paid. It doesn't mean you can't pay them on a number four day, and it doesn't mean that you must pay them on a number five day, but you'll be more in the mood on a number five day.

On your number six day, Venus day, circumstances are very good for emotional matters. You'll feel warm and loving and the people around you will feel the same way. That doesn't mean you can't make love on a number four day. It means if you make love on a number six day, you'll get more out of it. That's the day that you probably will be a little extravagant. You'll probably want to buy cosmetics or clothing. It's a luxurious day. But you can have that any other time, too, except that on the number six day its easier to be that way. You will love it!

On your number seven day, Uranus day, you'll feel drawn toward the higher philosophical approach, toward exploring the deeper meaning of yourself. It's a day when you might want to start on an extended trip. You may have unexpected situations happening, so on a number seven day you should be ready to meet any opportunity that presents itself. That doesn't mean you can't stay home and spend the day in bed or be all alone, but it's a shame to waste a number seven day. By being in front of a particular door at a certain time you might meet a very exciting individual, and it can develop into a beautiful relationship. It's a very jazzy, adventuresome day. You don't have to do anything with it, but it's there if you want it.

On your number eight day, which is a Mars day, you don't necessarily have to be in an angry mood or have arguments with everyone around you. Things are very dynamic and forceful. Forceful people tend to run into a little bit of aggravation occasionally. It's a very dynamic day, when you can assert yourself, unite your physcial, emotional and intellectual capacities, almost to the point of being dynamite in your environment. This doesn't mean it's an explosively bad day, but if you take your potential and put it to good use it can make a tremendous dent in your destiny in any direction you want. So number eight is a good day when you want to be very strong. It's also a good day for sexual contacts.

Number nine is a day of inspiration. It's a mysterious day. Mysterious things could happen, and if you are afraid to experience unusual events, you might stay home and make no move that day. Still, the day should be used to find yourself, the meaning of what you are, and to establish possible relationships that will have a hold on your life in a haunting, mysterious, melancholy way. Sometimes you may be tired on a Neptunian day. That doesn't mean you can't do any of the things that you can do on any other day. It's just that it will be easier to explore your spirit world on your ninth day.

You see, through witchcraft and its control and understanding, you are programming yourself to experience the full range of numerical life adventure. Knowing what the days offer in potential for you, you are in position to take advantage of all experiences. Every day can be your lucky day once you have mastered the formula.

# 7

# Letters to a Witch

> *"Everything happens to everybody ... sooner or later ... if there is time enough ..."*
> George Bernard Shaw

People always want to know something about themselves, their future, the answer to their problems. Too often, however, they want to be impersonal about it. They think that for two dollars anyone can tell them about their future. I would never bother. I couldn't care less for that type of personality. The world is full of loneliness, and sadness resulting from mixed-up lives. I can become very moved with the idea of sadness in people, but I can't always do anything about it.

Letters come to me by the hundreds, usually right after I have made a broadcast appearance. They tend to either ask for advice, information on how to cast spells, or, in some cases, just friendly correspondence. The friendly ones sadden me: Their reaching out towards a total stranger touches me. It must mean they have no one else to turn to.

As I exhibit a psychic ability on television shows and on two-way radio, people assume that I want to be a fortune teller! I do know things in advance, and I could be a fortune teller, but not every psychic is involved in fortune telling. There are people from all walks of life who are psychic—politicians, lawyers, doctors, businessmen, actors—but no one would dream of asking them for a reading—and surely not for two bucks.

When strangers write to most psychics, they get some kind of form letter back, signed, "Friend," and for so many dollars they will mean it! But to me that is the least friendly thing that can be done to lonely people, troubled people. I am friend enough to the strangers to leave them alone. I have enough respect for them as human beings. I'd rather the letter writer assume that I was a lousy person for not answering his letter than send a sickening-sweet form letter.

Difficulties arise in every life. But I don't think anything is all bad. There's some value in almost everything that happens. The thing is to find out where it fits. I really don't believe there is ever a wasted situation. Everything that ever happened to you did something for you. You got something out of it! You gain some kind of insight, even from terrible burdens. To control a problem and compensate for it, you excel in something else. If some people didn't have a little handicap, they wouldn't be what they are. I think everybody is great. Each individual is alive and unique and can offer something of value that nobody else can.

People write to me and many times use the letter to clarify their own thinking. There's nothing wrong with that if it helps them solve problems by spelling them out to a stranger. There are many problems beyond the care or practice of a witch. Why should legal cases, medical problems and financial advice be sought from a witch? Why not contact the proper authorities in the field?

I knew a prostitute who kept calling me for several years. She always wanted her fortune told and the question was always the same: "When is 'Mr. Right' coming for me?" I liked her. She was kind of delightful, charming, naive, and pretty. Like many prostitutes she began her career when she was about 12 or 13 years old. She had a strict, religious mother and an alcoholic father. She wasn't very smart. She kept having children. She was the kind of prostitute who would go to a party and get maybe one hundred dollars for the night, but there might be 50 guys to service. She always told me how she fell in love with every man she met outside of her work. She was always ready and waiting to fall in love, and every year she wanted to know if Prince Charming, who would love her for herself and want her to quit her line of work, would show up. But every man she met took advantage of her and would either knock her up, or put her to work for his own profit. A long line of no-good guys. Everybody took advantage of her: queers, pimps, convicts, everybody. She was constantly beaten up and abused. The poor girl was looking for true love, but in the wrong place, in the wrong world. She was never going to find it, never. She was unbalanced and psychiatry didn't help. How could I tell this girl that she was never going to meet a man who was the answer to her dreams?

But there are some answerable problems, questions dealing with witchcraft and common human problems that are typical of any cross section of America. These I can try to answer, even though I sometimes get impatient with the writers. These are real people who write to me, either as a result of television appearances, two-way radio broadcast programs, or through my syndicated newspaper column, "Sorcery, Spells, Symbols and Stars."

> Dear Scorpio,
> 
> *You may not be, as you stated so clearly in your letter, "enough Josephine for his Napoleon," but you should be credited with a gold star and a capitol E for the effort. Yes there are ways to determine emotional compatibility within the frame work of Astrology, but I am afraid I am at a loss to deal with this situation. According to Astrology the position of Mars and Venus in the two Horoscopes may be used as a basis for comparing the Male and Female qualities between the partners. However in the relationship you have outlined it is difficult to determine where one's Josephine leaves off and one's little Corsican begins. One cheering note: The Moon in your chart is in the same sign as the Moon in the other gentleman's chart, and this would suggest that*

*at least you do both have the same idea about women. Good luck.*

Dear May 23, 1926

*You neglected to explain if the straying male is your lover or husband. There are many spells that might be used to control the situation . . . but these vary depending upon the existing conditions. You might serve your lover and/or husband a parsley and zuccini soup seasoned with Mint leaves Basil. Some Witches say this works.*

Dear F.R.G. in Venice,

*Since you only suspect that the woman has taken some of your personal belongings, I suggest you begin with just a simple spell . . . just in case she might be innocent. Each day for nine days mail to her a bird's blue tail feather dipped in olive oil. However . . . if you ever discover her guilt for certain . . . call the City Attorney. If you still are not able to recover your possesions: Let a green candle burn for 77 days.*

Dear Stan in West Los Angeles,

*The fact that you have belonged to a Nudist Association for the past seven years is not going to help you get into a legitimate Witches Coven. Why do you stress that your interest in Witchcraft is not sexually motivated? And then find the need to brag that you are considered "pretty good." Since your letter states that you are 22 years of age . . . it seems to me that your attitude about your abilities stems from your emotional partners no doubt being rejects of some tired 70 year olds. Cool it baby. Cool it!*

Dear May the 4,

*I do not understand why you should have fainted while trying to cast the Emotional Bondage Spell. Before continuing with the herbs and incense perhaps you had better contact your doctor. Rosemary and Thyme are not* known for their intoxicating fumes. It could have been that the candle snuffed out the oxygen in the small enclosed area. Where were you anyway?

Dear Potential Witch (July 19, 1933)
Witchcraft is a disciplined activity. When casting spells rituals must be followed exactly if they are to have a powerful affect. You must use a copper bowl for the "Full Moon Ring." A pyrex dish will not do!

Dear H. D. (November 12, 1934)
From what you have written concerning your illicit romance, I am led to believe that you consider yourself to be a pawn and the innocent member of the love partnership. Perhaps . . . indeed . . . you are a 'victim,' but I would say more a victim of your own emotional and sensational appetites than of anything else. Why not try the Sex Watchers Plan and see if you can control the intake a bit . . . for the sake of appearances.

Dear Pisces (March 8, 1922)
All Witches and Wizards do not participate in Orgies. And yes, you are right . . . I won't give you a list of the ones planned for the Roodmas Festival in April . . . And NO . . . you can't become a Witch. Witches are female!

Dear November 26, 1928
Thank you for the lock of your hair. I do not feel like casting a spell in order to win back [your] lover . . . and so don't expect any improvement in that department to come from my direction. There is a way that you could attempt the project on your own. Try Head and Shoulders.

Dear Desperate Scorpio,
I am surprised that a sexy Scorpio like you has to resort to cry baby tactics. The Emotional Bondage Spell

has worked for others ... perhaps your error was in eating the head of garlic rather than wearing it. And please go easy with the red candles, they are very potent. Readers have written in that your spell ... has been affecting their relationships. Try Coral or Pale Pink.

Dear Passionate Pisces,
    When a reader writes in that they are never able to find emotional partners ... despite their fascinating attributes ... I question the validity of their gifts. Perhaps True Love Tea would help you ... but I doubt it ... and frankly ... K couldn't care less. However ... good luck!

Dear Louise:
I cast your "Sex Seduction Spell" on this guy I liked. Those spells work beautifully. Now he won't leave me alone. Tell me: Is there a way to remove the spell? I still like him, but I want him to love me for me and not for the spell, and I was wondering if I could cast spells for someone else. Is this possible? I'm not a witch but I've had psychic experiences. My birthdate is March 1, 1950. I hope you'll answer my letter soon. This guy is driving me crazy.
Sandy J.

    Well, I think Sandy, you're just thrilled to death that he's driving you crazy. You seem to like to be driven crazy. He does love you for you, and not for the spell. You cast the spell. What the spell did was accentuate what you are, and it is you that have done it. All you did was plant the essence of yourself in his subconscious, and he reacted to it. He liked you. So it's you; he's not being deceived. I'd recommend the unwanted lover spell, but that's not what you really want.

Dear Louise:
Can the powers of witchcraft be used to make money? For example, I know a man who is very rich, and I'd like to make him give me a $100,000. Is there any special way I can go about

this? He lives 400 miles away. Just exactly how can you live without working? You must have some way of making money. I'm a believer. So help me, I'm not evil-minded—just a groovy, all-turned-on person. I was born Jan. 6, 1948.

William S.

*First of all, I guess that if you wanted to cast a spell that psyched you up into believing you were influencing someone to give you money, then were so energetic that you could project your thought, I believe that you might be able to accomplish this. Whether or not you are able to do it is something else again. I doubt that you have that kind of dynamic personality that would enable you to project that. You're not strong enough. If you were so completely turned on to yourself, you wouldn't need a $100,000 gift—you'd have made it yourself. I think one can cast such a spell, but the situation would have to allow for it. You do not seem to me to be the person who could perform this money spell and make it work.*

Dear Louise:
My 14-year-old son has developed a psychological problem, and I am hoping you can give me some advice on the approach and possible outcome. He is highly intelligent, they say, but extremely withdrawn. His birthdate is November 22 and mine is December 5. I am in the process of arranging special schooling and counseling for him.

*The fact that you've written to me, a witch, indicates that you still wish what's happened, whether it's a physical thing or environmental thing, was not your responsibility. You're writing to me to hear that some other thing has caused it, like a hex, some evil spell. But you're starting counseling and are beginning to face up to the fact of what really made this happen. All of your family is involved. I feel you are writing to me because you want a mysterious reason why this kid is the way he is, rather than accepting the responsibility that this is something* that took place in your family. Turn to a psychologist, in this case, not a spell.

Dear Louise:
I want to use the "Sexual Seduction Spell" on a certain girl. I can't say that I love this girl, but I will say that I want her, and I'll do anything to get her. I want to know if there are any spells that could be used. Will you assist in any way you can? Also I would like to learn more about witchcraft, about practicing it. I'd like to know if you can make up your own spells or if they have to be set patterns. I was born May 19, 1950. Please don't take this letter lightly. I'm very serious about the whole thing.
Bob M.

> You do not love her, so what you want to do is overpower her to feed your ego, which is on very shaky ground. The first thing you should do if you want to use witchcraft is to start casting spells on yourself so that you will not need a situation where you must overpower someone. She will come to you because you are so absolutely devastating that it's the only course she can take. If you remain sick and inferior, casting spells won't bring any luck. The first spell you have to cast is the one to strengthen yourself. The spells are of equal intensity. It's you who should become stronger. You can make up your own spells if you are experienced and powerful through witchcraft. They don't have to have a set pattern, but you have to have a constant pattern once you establish it. Figure out a spell and stick to it. But that's not for novices.

Dear Louise:
I've been a widow since 1962 and I was born July 24, 1902. I want to sell this home and either move to Arizona near my sister or move near my 83-year-old aunt in upstate New York. Do you see me selling this place? And also do you see me meeting a nice man companion? I wouldn't get discouraged if you say no. Also, I'd like to go back to work. I am a beautician and a good one.
Harriet H.

*I don't believe you want to go live with your sister. I don't believe you want to go live with your aunt. I think you want to go live with a man. I think you would enjoy it very much. Judging from the tone of your letter, you have reached the point where your own frustration has an effect on your direction, but my reaction is that you are about to meet a man, very soon, because that's what you want to do even though you're not aware of it; that's your next step. Try true-love tea.*

Dear Louise:
My husband walked out. This is about the third time. He tells me he no longer loves me and wants his freedom. He has been unfaithful many, many times. All in all, I think he could be a good and wonderful person. I still love him. What do you see in the future for us? We have been married 19 years. My birthdate is January 8, 1924 and his is October 17, 1922.

Nora B.

*You have obviously operated for 19 years inside a comfortable pattern. He hurts you, then you love him in spite of it all, and it's very clear and simple to see that this is a pattern that's comfortable for you. Evidently he needs assurance that he'll be loved no matter what he does, and you enjoy the role of loving somebody who's not so nice, who's mean to you. You say, "I still love him." Well, that's questionable. I don't know what love is to you or to him, or if this is a love situation. You're not asking me whether or not you should separate, or whether or not he will change. You are telling me: "This is my pattern. I love a man who many times acts like he doesn't love me." This is the way you want to live. You are two people who feel inferior, each one doing something that balances out the other's feeling of inferiority. If you wanted to have a different kind of partner, there are all sorts of dynamic things that can be done in witchcraft to energize that part of your psyche so that you would find the proper partner. But you do not want the proper partner. You like him!*

Dear Louise:
I am writing to you to tell you that I think your show was the most fantastic thing on the air, and I truly believe in witchcraft. I wish very much that I was born a witch (June 2, 1953) but unfortunately I am not. I think, however, I have some sort of psychic powers. I mean sometimes I can hate a person so much and wish the worst thing on them, and it will happen. It has happened so many times that it has really convinced me of having the powers. Is there any way that I can control myself? I'd appreciate any help you can give me. Is there a shop where someone can go to purchase objects for spells? I heard of such a shop from someone. Where can I purchase a Mojo? I think you are really fantastic. I hope that some day I can meet and talk with you. Can you possibly give me a spell where I can make a person like me?

> *Poor kid. It's pretty sad when you have to feel you must cast a spell to make somebody like you. But you strike me as a free young spirit, and it's good you are seeking inner control, especially over hate. Hate is a waste of time. Better spend it casting spells to improve your own life. Try the "Self-Fascination Spell." While you're young it works better. There are so many psychic 16- and 17-year-olds today, it indicates there must be more psychic children being born. Being psychic is more prevalent in children, but by the time you're 16 or 17, you may not be. Babies are intuitive, and so are small children in nursery school, but usually by 16 and 17 the power is gone. It gets wiped out, suppressed, conditioned out.*

Dear Louise:
I have been told by many people who are knowing in the field that I am a witch. I also feel that I might be, but I can't find my powers; neither have I been able to find someone who could help me. Is there any way I can find out if I'm a witch? My birthdate is January 20, 1944. I would like to see you and talk with you. Would this be possible?

Ellen S.

> *I don't think you are a witch. It's not possible for you to be a witch and not know it, because when you're a witch you feel your energy; you feel your power. It may be that you could be helped with witchcraft so that you could become a more dynamic individual. A witch has nine dimples on her body. Besides dimples you must be psychic and project your emotions into your environment. Since you haven't done it, you're not a witch.*

Dear Louise:
I joined your psychic experiment on television and saw a man I don't know and had never met in my entire life. I concentrated on love, and love to me is a newborn child. This man appeared on the unused television channel as I concentrated, and later he called me. My phone number is unlisted. And he says that he too saw me on his television set. I asked him what image he was trying to project and it was the same as mine, a newborn child. I described him and he described me. He was born October 15, 1948, and I was born October 15, 1948. All males in his family are wizards and all women in my family have been witches, except for my grandmother and my mother. Yet since I was a small child, I've had strange powers. Could I be the one to begin a new cycle of future witches in my family? Also can the wizard and myself be on the same wave length mentally? One more thing I can't understand is that he called me from Paris, France. He spoke French, and I don't understand French, but I understood every word and he understood my English. What gives? I swear all of this happened. Strange things have happened, but this thing has me scared, and it blew my mind. This is too much. I can't shake the fear growing inside of me. I am not sure how I shall handle this.

Norma T.

> *You are lying to me and lying to yourself. You have a very active imagination. That's delightful. But I don't believe you. I do believe that these strange things [can] happen. I had gone for years having difficulty with baby-*

sitters, and I suddenly realized the reason I was having difficulty in getting babysitters was because I didn't feel comfortable about leaving babies. So each time I'd have some place to go, I would short circuit the thing so that I could not go out. It was out of my hands. The babysitter would, for some reason, not show up. Something would happen that was beyond her control and mine, supposedly. Then I faced up to my situation. I cast a spell that enabled me to get a [housekeeper]. In other words, I psyched myself into believing that from that moment forward I would not have babysitting problems, and I cast a spell to do this for myself. Immediately, the Sunday following the spellcast, the phone rang. Wrong number. A young girl said, "Hello, Ada?" I said, "No, this isn't Ada. Are you a housekeeper?" She said, "Yes." I said, "Do you want a new job?" She said yes. I immediately went and got her and I had her for over two years. She had been working for someone named Ida. She'd only been working a short time. She'd gone home for the weekend, and Ada was to pick her up. She called Ada, but she dialed my number by mistake. I believe that can happen. But I don't believe a man from France called you after seeing you on his TV set.

Dear Louise:
Could you tell me if my life will ever be happy, and my love life. I have been thinking about a man I've known since I was 16, and I love him deeply. The last I heard from him he is in Los Angeles. I would like to find if he is right for me. His birthdate is about March 15, and mine is July 12, 1933. Please tell me what the future holds for me. Right now I need someone to care for and someone to care and love me. I'm a very lonely old lady right now. Life is not worth living sometimes.
Helen P.

> *I note the fact that you are 36 years old, not an old lady but an adult, and you answer your question yourself. At first you say that you have been loving this man*

since you were 16, and you are an adult, full-grown female. Here you've loved someone since 16 and don't know if he's the one for you. On the other hand you let us know right away that you do NOT really love him. What you want is to be able to love someone, and it doesn't matter who. I think that you have never learned to love yourself, to feel yourself or know yourself. If the man were even interested, I would caution him against the relationship because you really don't know what love is. You want somebody to end your loneliness, instead of looking to yourself and generating some excitement inside of yourself. No, I would advise you to first make yourself over into a person who could have a love experience with someone else. I think that's the whole thing. When you're able to love somebody, then, because you give love, you get love in return. Only when you are completely involved with yourself, love yourself, and are aware of yourself, can you know what love is and offer it to somebody.

Dear Louise:
This year I had to leave my full-time job because of health reasons, mostly emotional. I was born August 28, 1930, and I have three children. My leaving work at this stage was beneficial as I eliminated quite a few problems. I spent too much time on other people's problems and tended to neglect my own family. Only now I find myself picking on my husband and throwing his faults up to him, which is the exact thing I want to avoid. I am very impatient with him lately, and I try to hold back, but I get an overwhelming urge to bawl him out. Right now we are not speaking but I know we will be tonight. We are both very forgiving and adore each other. I just feel very ornery lately because I finally realized my bad points. I changed them but I am still the same way.

Greta L.

*I don't believe you changed your bad points because you continue to react in the same way. I don't feel the* *question is whether or not you've changed. I don't believe that's the point.* I think the interesting point is that right now you are not speaking, and I think that "right now" has been like many other times when you haven't been speaking. You want to avoid facing life. I think the first step between you is not to look to who's wrong in the situation but how you are going to operate as a team. How are you to operate effectively? I don't believe in the negative approach. You spend tremendous energy bickering back and forth after what's already happened, what's already been said, and who is at fault. All of that energy should be converted into a dynamic situation, to make tomorrow happen. There is a tremendous dissipation that takes place in wallowing in misery. I don't know what the problem is, but I think you could spruce up your relationship by completely stopping and beginning new. I don't think you should drag on the burdens of before. Sever them completely. Try the "New Life Spells."*

Dear Louise:
Long before now I have wanted to meet a witch and have been thoroughly fascinated by the supernatural. I do have the unfortunate problem of not being born a witch. I was born November 4, 1952. I was wondering if some people are more or less receptive to spells and psychic powers than others. I am clinging to the thought that hidden forces are at work somewhere in the universe, and I believe that occasionally I can pick them up. The main reason for this letter is to inform you of a reaction to the Hollywood Bowl "Sexual Vitality Spell" you and all the audience tried to cast on the population. I was shocked. From July until September I experienced a sexual hunger so powerful and furious that it was frightening. It had never happened before except those months in such an overwhelming way. I thought you might be interested to know that your experiment was a success on me, for I don't know what else could have caused it. But very definitely it had an effect on my behavior. I even lost a boy friend because I was becoming too possessive. Sexual

starvation is a horrible feeling. It's very irritating. I hope this is the kind of reaction you were looking for. I wish you would write to me and let me know if I really have any basis for my belief that it was your spell. I don't think it would be wise for me to try your "Sexual Seduction Spell" because I have enough problems with that subject without adding a spell to it. However, it sounds beautiful and maybe I'll get my salt and candle out. I am a terribly ambitious person and am wondering if you know anything I could do to insure my success. How much of witchcraft can a normal, average American rely on?

Marla G.

*Well, first I would like to say I am surprised and of course pleased to hear that you are a normal, average American with an overwhelming sex starvation. We didn't cast a spell for people to become sexually starved but sexually vitalized. It probably worked. You probably are tuned in to psychic forces and are quite able to practice witchcraft, but I don't know just by your letter whether or not you yourself are psychic, but I think you can turn-on well. As much drive as you've got is going to make a dent in your society.*

Dear Louise:
I am one of your fervent followers. I want to know is there is going to be any change in all the bad luck I have had since 1968. 1969 was bad so far for me likewise. I sit here writing you with a broken ankle which for some reason doesn't seem to want to mend in a hurry. I was born September 30, 1921. I love people and I go out of my way to help people, yet I cannot for the life of me figure out how a person who is so compassionate, who spends many hours praying for others as I, a true born-again Christian, can possibly draw so much bad luck towards themselves. Is there any possible change for me in the near future? If I had any idea that it stemmed from my unhappy childhood I would surely try to seek out the best-known hypnotists and find out from my subconscious mind all that could possibly be blamed for all this unhappiness in my life. If you have any

suggestions to this view of mine, please tell me what you think. I am a person with a good mind and a willingness to take other persons' views. I only hope and pray all the misery will end and happiness will soon smile down. For I love all people, for I know they are God's servants. God bless you again. I remain God's servant.

                        Gladys S.

> *First of all, I am a witch and I have very strong and definite reactions to people and situations and letters. I dislike Gladys intensely. My initial reaction is that she loves no one, and that anything that she might do for someone is a compensation in order to prove to herself that she really loves them. If you love people, you don't have to do a damn thing for them except glory in their presence. You don't have to be giving of yourself to prove that you love them; you love them and you know it. So right there I react to that sentence about how she loves people and will go out of her way to help people. I do not think she is loving. Nor God-fearing. She is an unhappy woman who never, ever thought to get out of herself, and she is attracting bad luck, creating it like a complete and total loser.*

Dear Louise:

I have been waiting for some information on my ancestors from my grandfather. He said all he could tell me was that every few generations the women in our family are psychic because they're cursed, and then a break in the cycle occurs and not one woman will be psychic in any way for three generations. It's every three generations, never more nor less, that a very unusual thing happens to one of the women. It's strange. I was born May 30, 1951. I got your lucky charm but I'm afraid it will take quite a bit more. When I want a man, someone in the family warns him that I'm cursed and that scares every man away. I don't have one real friend to talk to, male or female. I've thought of death and suicide but that's not for this kid. It would cause a lot of pain for my people. I don't like to see people hurt, but why can't guys open their eyes and know this of me, that I never cause any harm or pain to anyone. Oh yes, the charm almost worked once until he looked into my eyes, and after that he made a hasty retreat. If he had walked any faster he would have been running. But 18 years of age and have had not one date, not even a school dance. I'm lonely. To quote my sister: "You'll never get a boy friend; face the facts, you'll die an old maid." I could write a thousand pages about my feelings. My grandfather says that it's really a grand gift instead of a curse an ancestor placed on my family. By the way, she was burned in England for being a very evil witch.

Lisa G.

*This is a very interesting letter because, number one, you're 18 and already an old maid, then, number two, you had a very evil ancestor who was a witch, yet you're writing to another evil witch for help. Right there is a contradiction in what you expect to have happen from evil witches. It's obvious that you have emotional problems that may be inherited along with any possible psychic powers. You need to seek some sort of counseling. When people believe that a curse has been put upon them, it often is they who are cursing themselves. I cannot advise any charms, spells or anything except getting some psychiatric help. Immediately.*

Dear Louise:
You seem like such a nice, friendly person from the television. I have two questions I would like to ask you and it would be great if you could answer them for me. I was born December 8, 1947. Can the "Sexual Seduction Spell" be cast on two persons who aren't present as the spell is being cast, and what changes in the spell, if any, are needed for this? Two, I make belts and wristbands out of leather on consignment through a shop. Is there a spell I could cast on the things I make that will charm people into buying them? If there is such a spell, would you tell me what it is and how to cast it? My things attract a lot of attention, and people admire them and say they are good,

but only a few buy. If I could charm my goods in such a way, maybe people would buy instead of talk. It would really be great if you could help me get moving faster. I'm getting hungry and I need money and some more leather.

George G.

> *You're a little bit timid, George. You've gone out of your way to tippy-toe around me and say the nicest things so that I won't react to you unfavorably. Now what you really need to do is cast a spell in order to be a more forceful and dynamic individual. Automatically your goods will begin selling. Regarding the "Sexual Seduction Spell" for two other people, I cannot understand why you're casting sex spells for other people, unless you're a broker. If you cast a spell, and you've got enough emotional energy going, you can project this thought out into the air waves. The spell can work without the people there. If you're casting a spell for two people, the whole point is that you are putting an idea in somebody's subconscious. But, timid George, if you can't move your leather goods as quickly as you would like, yet still have enough power to get two other people involved sexually, I'm kind of interested in your technique. I suggest first you sell your leather goods, and then bother about casting spells for other people. You haven't yet got any energy to spare.*

Dear Louise:
Perhaps I was not born a witch. I am sure if I were I would be already aware of it. But I am quite psychic about my friends and what amazes me more than anything is that I pick up vibrations and thoughts from other people. My mother is also this way. She has premonitions and dreams enough to scare you. However, I'm sure you get many letters from people telling you how fantastically psychic they are. That is not my reason for writing. I want to know if you could recommend any reliable books on how to develop the powers of my mind. Anything you might suggest would be appreciated, and if you have any moments

with really nothing much to do I would really love it if you could send me a few procedures for magic spells. Especially the recipe for "True-Love Tea." I can't quite say I believe in magic when it's practiced by anyone. If I believe in something strongly enough, it will come true, and I suppose that is magic in a sense of the word, don't you think? I may not be making much sense but I hope you know what I'm talking about. All I really want is to improve my powers of concentration and strengthen my psychic side. I was born March 10, 1954. About all I can tell you about myself is that I attend school, I am 15 years old, and I may sound normal, but you can be assured that I am not. I've been told many times that at least I'm definitely not normal according to average American standards. Perceptively yours.

Barbara H.

> *What good luck you had to have been born to a mother who would encourage this side of your mental behavior. To have reached that much insight at 15 about what makes yourself tick, I think maybe that you are a witch in the true sense of the word. The fact that a 15-year-old girl has such a good healthy relationship with her mother is a very nice thing for me to read.*

Dear Louise:
My husband has had an affair with another woman, and she gave birth to a child. I still love him and am willing to forgive him. I still want him back. He was born August 22, 1934, and I was born June 6, 1934. Should I take him back and will he end his straying if I do? He says he loves me. Will our marriage last?

Janet K.

> *I don't believe in forgiving when the person who is in a position to forgive probably contributed to the act in the first place. If you are forgiving your husband for reacting to something that you did to cause him to seek sex and affection elsewhere, well, who is forgiving what? Will your marriage last? It hasn't lasted. It is on the rocks. Try the potion for infidelity; then figure out what*

*the other woman might have given him that you did not, and serve generous portions of that, too. And if he alone is to blame, cast a spell to change him.*

Dear Louise:
I am dating two men who, strangely enough, have the same birthdays, April 18, 1942, and a lot of other similarities. Physical attraction is strong in both cases. I am 26, born June 1. What is my outlook for marriage and financial life in the next two years? Generally speaking, if you see any flaws in my personality, or any attributes and talents I should develop, please let me know.

Celia G.

*I'm amazed: You need a stranger you never met to point out if you have any serious flaw in your personality? And if I said you had some talent you'd automatically start developing it? All I know about you is that you apparently can write English and are 26 years old. Yes, Celia, I'm afraid you've got a flaw: not knowing that you have one.*

Dear Louise:
An astrologer did a chart for me (birthdate June 9, 1917) and nothing that was predicted has come true for this year. In fact, everything I attempt turns wrong. I've been going downhill in every way, shape and form. It's a nightmarish roller-coaster. To name just a few: Each record of mine that came out was a still-birth—not one single play, and my writing partnership was dissolved after four years, which means that I am a lyricist without a melody writer. My lifetime of attempts have come to naught. To finally face the reality that my lifetime has been in vain, and I am not one to kid myself, is hard. No male entered my life as the astrologer said. My health has been poor. In fact, the whole year that I had looked forward to so much has been terrible. There has been no bursting with creativity, no financial gain, no legacy. I'm baffled and sick at heart at the way everything happened to me just the opposite of what the astrologer

forecast. To not have even one of the good things happen and each day to see something else go wrong—I don't get it. I just don't understand. I am in tears.

Andrea G.

> You have the same birth date and astrological conditions as hundreds of persons who have been very successful. You obviously went to some astrologer and paid him to figure out what the planetary positions were at the time of your birth, and what these positions might mean by way of influence—what the conditions were. The planetary pattern indicated a period when you [could] meet men successfully, but only if you got out of the back room and into the sunshine outdoors! The planets won't shove him through the door. If you were looking for a man and a burst of creative energy at that time, you shouldn't have just sat back and waited on the skies. You can't blame a chart for not making your life happen. Positive action through witchcraft would be better, but even this requires you to act.

Dear Louise:
I'm not complaining, but it has been a very, very lonely life. Is there anything you can tell me that would help ease this life of loneliness? I am 77 years old, and so poor that I live on less than a dollar a day. I've had very, very many readings during my lifetime and enjoyed them all. I was born January 13.

Margie M.

> You are living on pennies a day, yet you admit spending what must have been many precious dollars for psychic readings and probably astrology charts and fortune tellings. It's your amusement; more than that you probably get friendship and a fantasy that things are going to be better. You feel you can buy friendship and hope from astrologers and fortune tellers. You don't want to know anything about the future; you know it is not going to change. You want somebody to tell you

# Letters to a Witch

*things that will be the things a friend would tell you to cheer you up, if you had a friend. My advice, find a friend. Don't buy fortunes.*

Dear Louise:

I am a widow, 64 years old come next November 14. I have had a rare friendship with a chap many years my junior, of eight years duration, which was broken up by a third party last year. I still have contact with this young man, who was born January 18, 1938, but the old basis, which included his driving my car in which we spent delightful hours enjoying scenery, has been disrupted. My question is, will this companionship ever be restored?

Esther F.

*How the hell should I know? And why should it? 33 years difference between you? I would be embarrassed to have a man that much younger, because I'd know that it wasn't my great sex appeal or charm that brought him to me. I'd figure it was a wet diaper! It's a sick combination. Why would you want to renew it? He smartened up; after eight years, you should. Some astrologer or fortune teller will tell you that you and this "chap" are fated lovers who met in a previous existence and will meet again and be happy in the next. Baloney! Try True Love Tea and a senior citizen's club.*

Dear Louise:

I have met a girl, a Pisces, who has a strange influence on me. I am Capricorn, January 5, 1947. She is not my type at all. Good looking in a way, but not the kind that arouses me sexually. I wasn't the least interested in her at first. Now I keep calling her all the time and trying to date her. I want to go to bed with her. It is strange because most of the time I don't care the least then all of a sudden I've got to have her. Could she be a witch? Has she put a spell on me?

John W.

*It's not easy to tell from what you say. It could be a witch if you meet someone, and there is a disturbance, and you feel haunted by them later. Of course that could also be called love. But if it did happen the way you say, there's a chance that the person you've met is a witch. A witch walking out of a room hasn't really left the room, and when that attitude still hangs there, you can be sure it's a witch. There will be a strong reaction one way or another. Whether you like this disturbance or not will depend whether or not you are repelled or enjoy this being. There's an energy. A lot of times it is mistaken for love. It's a psychic thing. However, it could also be that you and your subconscious don't agree on what's sexy.*

Dear Louise:
My husband and I talk openly on anything and everything. We praise each other, and we don't compete, as we each have our separate abilities, he with his electronics and me my art. We have our arguments—seldom—but in the next breath we carry on as though it never happened, and let it die a natural death. We love each other and understand each other, after ten years married. He caters to my desires and to my cycles, and when I see him bending backwards to please my moods, I am gratified to have such a thoughtful man and tell him so. There is one question in my mind though that I would like to know. We are both Leos, he born July 16, 1912, and I July 31, 1918. Can two of the same Zodiac sign be compatible?

Silvia N.

*You've been married to this man for 10 years. With all this experience behind you, you say you talk about everything and anything and love each other. It's a phony letter. You are really unhappy and trying to brainwash yourself into thinking everything's great. You're not in love. All these great things are going for you, but none of them are meaningful. You can put up with not being compatible if you're in love, if you're drawn together. Or you can have everything just down pat, but if there's no spark, it's not working. The trouble is, too many people are looking for the nice, neat, clean package rather than the spark. I think they're afraid to take chances with their emotions. They're not using their emotions. You're just living in a little storybook-type arrangement: You don't like him. An emotional rapport is missing. After going on and on about how compatible the two of you are, you ask me, a stranger, whether there is the possibility that the two of you could be compatible, which indicates just how much is lacking in your relationship. And why—why should [he] always bend over backwards?*

Dear Louise:
I was born October 16, 1922, in Prague, Czechoslovakia. Could you please tell me if I shall sell my property in the next few months? Will my health improve as I went through a bleeding ulcer operation and now my heart's giving me trouble? If you will tell me, I am not poor, and I pay you.

Myra M.

*I think it's very sad, but you're one of thousands of people who don't know where to turn. First of all, the kind of questions you asked me, should not be asked of a witch. You should go to yourself, your doctor, your attorney, a friend. I'm not your friend, attorney or doctor, and I know nothing about real estate. How can I tell you anything? What can I base my counselling on? The day you were born? No one would create a horoscope to such an extent as to be able to give advice on health and money as a special service. I couldn't possibly do this logically. The time involved is too expensive for you and me. It comes out to me that you are lonely and have no friends. Some people are braver in forming emotional relationships than with their money, and some people are braver with their money than with their emotional relationships. There's an imbalance there. They're fearful they're going to lose their security, and that alone should tell them to go get advice from the proper source. Obviously they're afraid that they're going to be destitute. Going to a witch, I should think, would be a very brave move. So, you have property, or money, and you have bravery. Why be alone?*

Dear Louise:
My mother has a psychic gift of some kind. She gets very definite feelings about whether we should be careful or not in relation to certain dealings, and sometimes just in our daily activities. At first we made fun of her, but later we found out that she was quite serious, and the results happened just about the way she said they would. What I would like to know is this: Does the future hold any positive gain in monetary rewards in the near future for me. I am 25 and mother is 52. She was born June 18 and so was I!

David W.

*It's kind of a sad thing at 25, because I don't think that's the age where you should be interested in establishing security, unless you just want cash to cut the apron strings. You should be seeking all kinds of keen sensations from a variety of experiences, as your primary concern, and not give a damn about the future, if there's any money coming in or not. The fact that your mother is psychic might make her a stronger impression on you than a person whose mother is not psychic. You write like a girl. I don't say you're queer, but you're not asserting your masculinity. I think if you're having a grand time with your life completely, somewhere along the line you're going to be able to make do. I don't think anybody who's having a good time is starving. The time poverty sets in is when you're not doing anything, when you're frightened and when you're hiding out.*

Dear Louise:
Do you believe in turning the other cheek? My birthdate is November 4, 1942. A German Shepherd of my neighbor's at-

tacked my small daughter and myself. I got nerve damage to the right leg as a result, so I sued against the neighbor and the insurance company. The next meeting is delayed to February. My neighbor says no good person would ever sue her, no matter what, but she won't even pay the doctor bills. She thinks I'm the most evil person on earth. She swears she'll keep canceling out until I forget about the suit. What do you think of my chances of settling my suit? I'm in pain for the rest of my life. Am I evil to sue?

Irmgarde C.

> *We've got a couple of sick neighbors here. The lady next door with the German shepherd is understandably not wanting to be sued and is trying to browbeat the passive neighbor into thinking she's evil. Well, witches are supposed to be evil, too, if you listen to just anybody. But if you have physical damage done to your body, and if you are wanting to know from a witch whether or not you should sue the people who caused the damage, you have some other kind of problem that needs doctoring, too. What is this difference between evil and good that people have such rigid concepts about? Is life a matter of little boxes; this is good, this is evil? It's ridiculous. There is no good; there is no bad. There's energy. And troublesome neighbors, and scars.*

Dear Louise:
I am 50 years old, born July 26, 1919, and the only way that I can get close male friends is to lie about my age. So I tell everybody I'm 40. I can get away with it on looks, but I get so nervous someone will find out that I sometimes shake all over. Will he leave me if he finds out the truth?

Sheila B.

> *So you want to know if you can drop 10 years and get away with it? Makes me think everybody's lying about their age. I was wondering why this girl who says she is 27 looks 20, until I realized the reason is that*

women who are 35 are saying they are 27, so this real 27-year-old looks 20. Anyway, you are lying about your age because you say it's the only way you can get close male friends. What kind of closeness is that? If you've got a close friend you can be 80 and have this thing going. You'll never get a [close] friend that way. As for the shakes, you are 50 and I'll bet you anything you're going through change of life, so if you're feeling frightened, go to a doctor. As for lying, you should never lie unless it serves your purpose. There's nothing wrong with honesty by itself, either. I believe that anything that might enable you and somebody else to have a good relationship is necessary and anything else is none of their business. Honesty is often used as a mask, a coverup for insecurity. But why lie if it makes you insecure? Better still, why not convince yourself, through witchcraft, that you are 40?

L.A. County Official Witch
Miss Louise Huebner
c/o United Western Newspapers
Dear Miss Huebner, Please let me say first that this is not a rude letter, or a letter meant for anything but to prove in my mind that there is a slight chance of your really being a Witch. First let me say, I was surprised to hear of your being the official Witch for the County, as I have never known a 'real' Witch to consent to publicity. I have known a few, when I was in England for a few years. I got to know two gypsies quite well. There are a lot of Witches who aren't psychic. I understand that Witches don't have to be psychic, and or if you are psychic, you don't have to be a Witch. (Peter Hurkos doesn't claim to be a Witch) When you are not born a Witch you must be ordained at the age of seven. Were you born a Witch or ordained at seven? If you were . . . you know your heart is BLACK! (not in color . . . it is still red like everybody elses . . . but it is symbolically black) And it will take 3 years to repent and become a someone else who isn't a Witch. Please if you don't mind, I would like to ask a few questions, if you are really a Witch you will know the

answers. If you don't know the answers I would believe you could be a Witches Apprintist.
1. Who was the Circle of Corinth?
2. What is the Blasted Hearth?
3. Who was Gauffridi? Charlotte Gadiere?
4. What does this mean: The Last Act of the Witches Sabbeth? and Talkmongers.
5. What is this?

and last but not least:
What does this mean to you:
Grand Bois, Carrafour, Cematiere, Damballah. These are just a few things every good Witch should know. Of course they would know the [WITCHES SPELL OF HATERED.] Most people think Witches are stupid or sick but they are neither ... They must know a great deal about spices and herbs so they can cure. Witch is of course what started Witchcraft. I guess you must know quite a few cures like: What good is Mandrake? or Passion Flower? I hope that you will not be displeased with my questions.

Sincerely,
Alice in Venice

P.S. I do agree with what you say in the papers about phonies and such. PEACE!

> Dear Alice in Venice,
> I'm so glad you explained that your letter is not rude. For a few seconds there I suspected that it might be, and I would be forced to HEX you, but then Witches often jump to conclusions and are known for their nervousness and irritability. So thanks for quieting my fears. Your surprise that a 'real' Witch would consent to publicity amuses me. Evidently you don't realize that 'real' Witches are a power mad bunch, clutching and clawing

at any and all opportunities that might place them into the limelight. As to being able to be a Witch without being psychic; That is absolutely ridiculous. If a Witch can change things... make things happen... do magic ... then she must be able to project a tremendous energy into the atmosphere. If she can project... she is psychic. If she can project she can receive. If she can receive she is psychic. Witches are psychic! Witches who are not psychic are cop outs.... Cop outs are phoney.

What do you mean Peter Hurkos doesn't say he is a Witch? Why should he? I for one would be terribly disappointed to find out he was masquerading in Drag. Peter so far as I am able to determine, appears to be a red blooded, true blue, virile male. Witches are generally understood to be female!

As to whether I was [born] a Witch or [ordained] a Witch at seven: I was born a Witch and am a sixth generation Witch. My mother is a Witch. My grandmother is a Witch. My grandmother's great grandmother was a Witch. I was not ordained a Witch at seven. I didn't get started on sex until a bit later.

For a minute I got a little jumpy when you said my heart was BLACK... but was relieved when you said the color is still red. I quit smoking six years ago and thought maybe that hadn't been any too soon! Besides BLACK is beautiful baby. Why in Heaven's name (if you will pardon the expression) should I ever care to repent three years... only to become a someone else who is not a Witch? I like being a Witch. As a Witch I am cuter, sexier, smarter, happier, more popular, more powerful, and continuously sought after by the cutest, sexiest, smartest, happiest, more popular, more powerful males in town. I see no reason to give all this up... just to be a someone... who is only a someone else. I am easily bored but you do idly entertain me with your ignorant curiosity. So I shall trouble myself for a moment to answer some of your questions.

*I don't know any Witch who I would want to be an Apprentice to! If you really met a few Witches in England you would have noticed they are a mean and violent lot . . . and very ornery to their Apprentices. Especially to their Apprentices. Most Witches I know become Witches immediately and would never ever bother to go through the Apprentice stage. As to the two gypsies you met in England. Forget gypsies. They are dumb and stupid and have nothing to do with Witchcraft. And now to your questions:*

*1. I don't know who the Circle of Corinth might be . . . but I could put you in touch with a couple of jazzy fellows in New York who hang around the Columbus Circle.*

*2. Sorry, I have heard of some faint hearts . . . but never a Blasted One!*

*3. As for Gauffridi and Charlotte Cadiere . . . I prefer to make no comment. Besides I had nothing to do with them anyway.*

*4. The Last Act of the Witches Sabbeth and the Talkmongers have me stumped too. But, you might check with Jesse Unruh and see what he can come up with.*

*5.*

*I'd say thats the Star of David with an arrow going through it.*

*And last but not least . . . . . : If it's O.K. with you I would just as soon not incriminate myself concerning the Grad Bois, Carrafour, Cematiere, and the Dambballah. Are you sure you won't settle for the Griffith Observatory, Pershing Square, Forest Lawn and the Los Angeles City Hall?*

*I guess by your description I am not a very 'good' Witch! But, if what you say is true about most people thinking all Witches are stupid or sick . . . then I guess you would probably qualify for the role quite easily.*

*Oh . . . Gee . . . I almost forgot! MANDRAKE: I guess he is good for something . . . but I certainly wouldn't want my kid sister to marry him. And as for PASSION FLOWER: They kill whatever is growing nearby . . . but are excellent for attracting flys and things.*

*Hope I have helped you set things straight.*

*Sincerely,*
*Louise Huebner*

*P.S. PEACE!*

# 8

# The Ways of a Witch

> *"My mother says*
> *I must not pass too near that glass...*
> *she is afraid that I will see...*
> *a little Witch that looks like me..."*
> Sarah Morgan Bryant Piatt

What's it like to be a witch in the modern-day world? If someone says she is a witch, there are many ways in which to react:
   1. She really is!
   2. She is lying!
   3. She thinks she is—and since there is no such person—she is crazy!
   4. She knows she is not—but thinks you are crazy!

A real witch doesn't care what people think about it, because what they think doesn't change what is. A witch doesn't behave obnoxiously, going around and declaring she is a witch, at a local church meeting, for example, just for the shock value, any more than witches fly about scaring people on Halloween. Why go about making people in your society unhappy or upset —without a reason? On the other hand, witches do not hide out in dimly lit rooms, seldom emerging. Personally, I am very much accustomed to public exposure. I speak at numerous club luncheons and am the center of attention for thousands and thousands of people when I do two-way radio broadcasts for four hours at a time. I was the first astrologer in the United States to broadcast on a large, metropolitan station, and my newspaper column has been read by millions.

Witchcraft is my method of doing things, the way I operate. It is a *modus operandi*. A witch is a female who is able to understand your thoughts, read your emotions—to be psychic —and yet, not only receive thoughts but send them, project emotion and change destiny. A witch is not passive; she is an activist.

My husband knows I'm a witch. With reason. We've had a lot of weird things happen to us, and I've told him in advance many things that are going to happen. He knows I'm psychic. He knows that I pick up things before they happen and that I'm somehow aware. There is a metal piece on the gate that jingles when anyone comes in. Sometimes I hear the jingle, and I go to open the door, but my husband isn't there. So I put dinner on anyway, and in no more time than it takes to drive up the hill, maybe 10 minutes later, he arrives. And, you can figure how it happens: As soon as he reached the bottom of the hill, he had the mental reaction, "Well, I'm home," and I would pick this up.

Maybe it will sound just too, too typical of a witch, but I DO live in a haunted house. We have all sorts of manifestations. One ghost that's almost always around is a child-sized one who for some reason always stands just a few feet from the piano in our living room. There is nothing to see, just the strong odor of decaying roses, which has been present off and on for years in this particular spot. Many people notice it and ask about it. We have no roses in our garden, but there were some, years ago.

The house was built by a man who lived in it for years with his family. It sits high in the Mount Washington area northeast of downtown Los Angeles, surrounded by tangled vines and foliage. We know that there were three violent deaths in the family who previously resided there, in close succession, shortly before we moved in. There are many unusual things about the house. We had to remove two doors to rooms inside because they wouldn't stay open. As soon as anyone would enter the room, the door would slam, and it created such a disturbing influence we had to remove them.

Other ghosts haunt our home too. One persistent ghost comes to mind in support of the belief that such projections may be uncontrolled energy bursts from a restless, living mind also occupying the house. The ghost appeared for the first time shortly after the family returned home from travelling through Europe. A series of hardships beset us: sickness, storms, and the like. Each of the children came down, one after another, with one childhood disease after another, and I got all of them in turn. Finally I came down with mononucleosis and was forced to stay in bed for a long period of time, which was difficult for me because I am rarely sick and am always active. My husband discovered the ghost. He was the first. He used to start out the day very early to get ready for work. While he was shaving, he was accustomed to hearing the children going by on their way to the front room to watch the early morning cartoons on television. One morning, a little bit TOO early, he heard something shuffling from the children's bedroom down the corridor, and he assumed it was the kids; when he called out to them, however, and then investigated, no one was up; no one was in the front room, no one was stirring. It continued to happen every day, so that he could listen carefully and distinguish a definite shuffling noise, and the direction it took. There was no explanation for it, except that it disappeared after I regained my strength. Our guess was that the noises were an extension of my own psyche, which in sickness I was no longer controlling. In addition to the shuffling, there was frequently a noise like a deep sigh, exactly the kind of sigh I frequently use when exasperated. I think the ghost was me, my wild, restless, uncontrolled unconscious, roaming around free.

Another ghost, manifesting itself in a completely different way, often appears in our doorway. Because our home is high in the hills and cut off from visibility by heavy foliage and trees, light cannot reach this area of the house. There is no way, not even from an airplane, that light from the outside could penetrate the point where this happens. But out of nowhere, there are little explosions of light, child-sized, sometimes taking the shape of a cone. The flashes come and go with equal mystery. No reflections, no prisms could cast that burst of light. We always check and find nothing. Many of our friends have witnessed the phenomenon and are mystified.

Speaking of lights, I remember that when we were on the road driving in Italy one night I suddenly screamed and told my husband, "Watch out, there's a truck!" Well, there wasn't a thing on the road in our lane, but because I had screamed that there was a truck in our lane, he pulled over to the curb, as far as he could go, and at that split second, a truck came up over a hill, straight at the lane where we had been driving. That's a kind of ghost, a ghost of a truck.

My mother had many psychic experiences. I recall one night a woman who had been a madam had been found strangled, and the story appeared in a New York newspaper. My mother felt, in a dream-like vision that night, that the murdered woman came to our home and told her that she had a daughter that nobody knew about, and that somebody had to help her because her life was in danger. My mother woke us all up, and we tried to figure out what to do, but my mother did not know this woman or anything about her except what had been in the paper. There was nothing we could do. The next morning, the daughter was found dead in a distant city, she had committed suicide. The discovery of her body was the first indication that the woman had a daughter.

I think we are all tuned-in to a wild energy-life impulse, and that sometimes something inside us understands a vibration that is outside of us. Or perhaps our inner mind understands the vibrations from all around us at all times, but only lets us become aware of them when there is danger or excessive energetic emotion.

My mother, who is a very powerful witch, has a special spell that I call her "Goodbye Spell." If you meet her, and if she doesn't like you for some reason—maybe she doesn't like your attitude toward her, for example, you'd better be prepared to travel. People she doesn't like go on her get-rid-of list, and she's very successful at it. People on this list just all of a sudden lose their jobs or decide to move thousands of miles away. Somehow they are just removed from the area. After being in one place for 10 or 20 years, they're gone in two weeks after she puts them on that list of hers.

We had one neighbor who lived just a little way down the hill; she was a terrible bother and a real annoyance to me. I projected the thought that she would be out of the neighborhood in two weeks. And she was. Now you can say that what really happened was that perhaps I picked up telepathically, through her subconscious, the fact that she already had plans to leave, and that triggered me into casting a spell for her to leave. I won't argue. But the truth is—she did leave!

Witches are very self-centered and consequently don't waste much time casting spells against other people. We are not so much concerned with somebody else failing as with ourselves succeeding. If you fail as a by-product of my success, that's something else again. But I'm not going to waste energy trying to knock you down. So I find it difficult to believe that most of the people who think they are hexed by witches really are. They may be just hexed by themselves, and a good way to get rid of that is to start casting spells in another direction.

Once, however, I felt that a woman I knew had been malicious long enough. It so happened that she was a member of a group of couples that were going to dinner one night. Well, another witch and I decided we would work a spell that would give the woman stomach cramps that were strong enough for her to leave the table at 9 p.m. At exactly that time, she got up from the table and ran to the john. Later, she mentioned she had severe stomach cramps—out of the blue. So once in a while I fool around, but to sustain a hex takes so much energy that I could use elsewhere, I just don't want to be bothered. I'd rather spend the time psyching myself and projecting constructive emotions.

Many primitive people don't want to have their picture taken. Just an old superstition? Well, I had a spell worked against me by some crazy witches a few years ago, and they used a photograph of me to concentrate on. Their idea was to plant in me the seeds of self-destruction. My mother was in New York, and while there, she visited some psychic friends. Friends and family—all of them had a feeling that something was being done to me. Everyone said they believed someone was trying to hex me. What happened, actually, was that I was getting extremely rushed. I didn't attribute it to witchcraft. I just thought I was becoming involved in hectic situations for other reasons. When you are rushed and you're nervous, you seem to do everything wrong, and then other things go wrong and all parts of your life are affected as a consequence. You're not at your best, and in the end you're bound to slip up. The idea of the hex is to get you into a nervous state, then depressed and to the point of feeling that nothing is worthwhile. I was getting a bit jumpy. A dog came along and had eight puppies on the front door step. The cleaning lady who came to the house twice a week, who didn't know anything about the psychic's warnings, kept telling me that something was wrong with the house. She insisted that some kind of wind was blowing through the house; she would go from one end of the place to the other cleaning and by the time she was done, the "wind" had disrupted everything behind her. This is interesting, because if those witches were affecting only me and my own self, getting through to me and making me feel funny, how could they get through to me enough that objects in my home could be manipulated? Newspapers and magazines were flying about; clothes were falling off their hangers.

My mother called me from New York that night and asked what was going on. Then she suggested the witches we knew should get together immediately, not in the same place, of course, but at the same time, in order to concentrate on whatever force was coming in, repel it, and send it back to where it came from. We cast a spell. The whole situation cleared up. Everything righted itself.

Later I discovered, via the Mandrake Vine, that a woman who couldn't stand me had taken my photograph, and she and some people who were studying witchcraft concentrated on my photograph every day and attempted to plant havoc in my life. Was what happened just our imagination? I doubt it. We had felt all the strange things happening before I had heard from my mother and friends sensing the spell against me. So what was it? Could the spell have caused such chaos in my subconscious that I was creating disorder everywhere in the house?

Witchcraft, from my point of view, is not supernatural, but it certainly is a supernormal activity. It's the way I operate. For me, being a witch is a way of being. Witchcraft is not a talent; it's a method. Being psychic is a condition that could exist for anyone. I am psychic. I utilize witchcraft. I do shows demonstrating what I do, but I'm also a good publicist. I write. I even sing. And many people in various professions also do this. Many fortune tellers are not psychic and not witches. Some people are sensitive, some are not. Being a witch is one facet of what I am, not my entirety.

Some people figure that, with a psychic grasp of the future, I should spend all my time at the race track, making big bets to get rich. Well, there are other, steadier ways to get ahead in life. Being psychic would help me whether I was a dancer, singer, or worked in a bank. Many lawyers practice witchcraft but are not fortune tellers and don't go to the races. Many singers enjoy singing and make money at it incidentally. Why, then, should I go to the races just because I'm a witch?

As a witch, I enjoy establishing a psychic rapport with someone. I do it quickly, and I have become addicted to the sensation, just as people who enjoy making love keep attempting to recreate the experience. The radio offers me, through two-way contact with the public, a delightful supply of psychic stuff —for me to "rapport."

When people ask if I get together with other witches and I say, "No, very rarely," they want to know if there is competition between witches. My answer is that I'm not competitive with a witch who is a housewife but I would be competitive with any woman who was after a job I wanted, witch or not. For instance, I like doing radio and television shows, and I would compete with a woman who was after the same show I wanted. Witchcraft is not my profession, although it is rapidly becoming something like that. I am me, and I have nothing in common with any other witch. If I were not a witch, I'd probably be singing or dancing or doing anything I could to get in front of an audience. It just so happens that I'm a witch.

Many witches on the lunatic or fake fringe advocate doing their stuff very hush-hush, but I don't have the kind of personality to do things secretly. I know some women who practice witchcraft, keep quiet about it, and worry that they might someday surprise their husbands. I don't keep quiet about anything, not even about being a witch. I'm not quiet about my political or religious views so I'm not likely to be quiet about that. Most witches I know make no bones about it, and everybody knows what they are.

When I was a teenager I worked at fortune-reading parties. They were like the Tupperware parties of today. One woman would invite 10 or 15 others who would pay for their reading, and the hostess would get her fortune told free. One day a woman came through the door of the kitchen, where I was doing these readings one at a time. The minute she walked through the door I looked at her and became so sad that I could not stop crying. Tears just poured out of me. She sat down at the table with me, and I was terribly embarrassed. I said, "I'm awfully sorry, but I feel so overwhelmed with sadness that I don't know what's wrong with me." She said, "That's right; you've got it right," and that was my reading for her. She sat there crying, and I sat there crying with her. I never said another word, and after a half hour she got up and went into the other room and told everybody I was marvelous. I felt such an immediate rapport with her that her whole life had hit me, and I was so overcome that there was nothing to say. Later I heard that she had had many ghastly things happen to her; she had a horrible life. I had never seen her before, but somehow I could feel it. I could not have told her the specific things that happened to her, but I was drowning in sorrow. I've always been very good at getting this type of psychic impression—something emotional that concerns the person I am in contact with. But it doesn't always work.

I remember another woman who came to me, and I threw the cards out for a reading. Suddenly I became immobilized and did not want to give her a reading. She demanded, "Well, aren't you going to tell me anything?" I said no; I just told her I didn't feel like it. She got up and left and just then I did get an impression: I visualized her grabbing somebody by the throat and choking him to death. I gave several other readings that night. The party was soon over and forgotten, but about a week later the hostess called me and said I certainly had disturbed the woman I had refused. The hostess said, "She said if she ever sees you again, she'll choke you to death." I have never lied in a reading. I have never made up or changed things I felt. But I have many times refused a reading, and I don't care how people react; I just don't believe that some things should be brought up, and maybe encouraged to happen. I feel that we're not really sure what takes place between two people in a situation like that. We know that there is an exchange of ideas and thoughts, but if I'm picking up something from you, I'm not really sure it's a thing that you have in your subconscious that you want to do or plan to do. Maybe you feel consciously you shouldn't do it, and maybe there's every good reason why you shouldn't; maybe it's something you will never do, but have strong feelings about. Sometimes I pick things up that really are going to happen that nobody knows about, but there's really no way to distinguish what it is that is received mentally.

So it must be considered just an intriguing experiment in telepathy to tell someone what they're thinking and feeling, but just because I tell you what you are thinking and feeling doesn't mean that you should race out and do it. That's a problem a witch runs into all the time.

One woman called, and I immediately felt very strongly that there was something that would take her back east. She asked me, "Should I go east?" I said, "Are you in a position at this time to go back east?" She said she was. I said, "Do you have enough money to do this?" Again she replied affirmatively. I asked, "Do you have any ties here to keep you from going back east?" She said she did not. I asked, "Do you want to do it?" She said yes, she did. I told her, "Well, if you want to do it, and you have no ties here to keep you from doing it, and you can afford to do it, do it." She said, "Should I?" I said, "Yes." She said, "God bless you!"

Actually I told her nothing she did not know or feel, just cleared up what was in her mind, what she felt. That's not giving advice, to point out what she desired. She was very thankful, but *I* didn't send her east: She wanted to go. I'm in favor of people doing what they want to do when they can do it.

A witch constantly gets impressions of a telepathic nature. When I was driving home, recently, I was very depressed about a dress that a seamstress had just turned out for me. It looked very ordinary, and what's the sense of getting a dress made if it's going to look like any dress you can buy off the rack in a store? On the way home I was thinking that I should find somebody who is a competent seamstress but who has no need to be a designer; that way I could design my own clothes without having to sew them. Finding somebody who only wanted to sew was the problem. It was about 6 p.m., and while driving on the freeway this thought was very strong. I decided to call my sister, who lives in another town, and maybe there find someone. So I called her at 9 p.m. and asked if she knew a seamstress. She said she would call a friend the next morning and then call me back. Instead, my sister called to say that the seamstress had called *her!*

Now, that's understandable. I had talked to my sister, and we had put a thought out together between the two of us. The woman was probably contacted telepathically and called because she thought my sister wanted her for something. However, the woman said she hadn't started to think about my sister at 9 p.m. Rather, she had started to think about her at 6 p.m. She heard my sister's voice call her at that time and believed that something had happened. Her husband had told her it was just her imagination, but she was impelled to call early Sunday to see. That means she didn't pick up the thought because we were talking about her; she picked up the thought at 6 p.m.—before I even knew she was the woman we were going to get in touch with! That's a different kind of a psychic thing.

My sister has a mysterious psychic link with all other members of the family. It frequently happens that I have the urge to telephone her but postpone the call because it might be a time of day that she is busy with her children—or maybe it will be too late in the evening. When this happens, when I want to talk to her but for some reason do not, she *hears* me talking in another room of her house. She hears a mumbling and knows it's me. So *she* telephones *me* and says, "What is it you want?"

This strange power extends even further: Whenever any member of the family dies, that member will appear to her, in her home, exactly as they are. So if an older member of the family, someone we know to be physically far away, walks into her house late at night, we fear the worst. Invariably an emergency telephone call comes later to inform us of the death. We gulp and say, "We know."

There seems to be no end to the mysterious things that happen every day in the life of a witch. But who knows, perhaps the strange things are not inexplicable, perhaps they could happen to everybody, except that most people are not attuned to the sixth sense, the extra sense, the way witches are.

Whenever there is an unusual happening in my life, I try to explain it to myself in terms of psychic energy. Somehow out in the air that separates, and yet connects, all human beings, like water links all fish to one another, something is able to travel between us. We don't know enough about the nature of energy and the power of the mind to refute this possibility, and the sometimes amazing cases of extra sensory perception that occur and which scientists have verified, speak volumes in favor of the strange phenomena.

The thing that most persuades me to adopt this theory of the existence of another force beyond everyday experience is the feeling that comes over me when I am giving psychic impressions of complete strangers. All I know for sure is that when I talk with them I feel united with them. Not in a spiritual or brotherly sense—but in a joyful sense similar to love. I feel we have blended our personalities for an instant.

There is no touch, no word, no thing, so what has made this contact? What is that invisible thing that happens? If such a mental contact can be made between any two people, then there must be a whole world of unexplored communication that lies beyond the horizon of the mind, waiting to be explored. And since it is a bond between humans, not unlike love, it seems very desirable that we do explore it.

# 9

# Witchcraft and You

*"Around the world thoughts shall fly...
in a twinkling of an eye..."*
Martha "Mother" Shipton

Now that the secrets of witchcraft have been revealed, and explained, you can see that there is magic there, and it is none the less mysterious or powerful because you can understand what makes it work. People have always feared that which they do not know, so it may be of some comfort to realize that there is at least a possible explanation for even the strangest of things.

We have looked at the false ideas about witchcraft and witches stemming from the past, and we can see that it was fear —fear of mysterious occult powers and the ultimate of terrors among superstitious people, fear of the devil—which led to innocent people being hung and burned as witches in a panic spurred on by individuals using witchhunts for their own selfish and evil purposes.

The solid, serious foundation of witchcraft from its earliest practice by men of medicine and science also has been pointed out. And it has been noted that the churches, too, employed similar objects and rituals to achieve the same effect as witches do: the flame of candles, the ringing of bells, the Book, soft music, chants, statues, soft fabrics, and flowers were part of a whole experience that people ages ago first discovered in their churches and were keyed up into feeling the full awe of religion.

What the witches did, of course, was take these objects and influences home, using them in their own private lives to achieve a fullness of respect for life, and to attain their own hearts' desire —with a few personal prayers or chants thrown in along with several little things and rituals the churches never thought of. But in the same way that religion gears itself to an after life, witchcraft aims to improve *this* one.

The close relationship between witchcraft and human emotion is inescapable to any student of the art, which cannot be called a black art unless you call all emotion evil. What most people want most is an emotional experience, and whether they seek it on the sexual level or in some pure, spiritual and romantic sense, witchcraft can open up the way to finding it. Encouraging your own innermost emotions whatever they may be, fanning the flames of your inner self is part of the principal business of witchcraft.

Freeing your own untapped powers through spells and chants, and glancing into the future and changing it to suit your wishes, these are the ways of a witch. Recipes, fortune-telling systems, the whole pattern for a better life through witchcraft is in your eyes and on your lips.

Those who find dealing in witchcraft strange, something that will set them apart from their fellow man ought to review the widespread observance of superstition among all peoples of the world, rich and poor, young and old. All superstitions are traced back to meaningful ideas or customs. Like witchcraft, they survived because they *did* have meaning. Unlike witchcraft, most of their true meanings have been lost down through the generations.

You don't have to look very far to find some phases of witchcraft used in today's world. Even the Pennsylvania Dutch, who are considered very good, highly religious people, use a form of witchcraft. They use strange writings and hexes on their barns and over their doorways to protect them from things considered evil, and to promote good.

Everything changes in time. There is nothing that exists today that existed in the same exact form a few hundred years ago, and witchcraft is no exception. In the same manner that ancient fortune-telling cards have become an alluring gambling game that whets men's appetite for money in the instant future —with the turn of a card—the rituals and spells of witchcraft have been altered by time.

Once you become powerful enough in casting spells that other witches have found successful in the past, you will find yourself able to adapt them more to your individual needs. It must be stressed that it takes a very strong personality to create variations on the tried and true, but so long as the principle is there, the clear self-assurance of what is going to happen as the result of the spell and the repetition, it will work.

The witch has always been an innovator, ahead of her time, able to see things that others did not see, unafraid to explore a source of power beyond normal comprehension. But normal comprehension and normal powers have changed with time, too. For instance, think about colors. The color concept is a comparatively new one. Ancient man did not understand color as we know it today and was unable to respond to the high-frequency electromagnetic pulsations. Certain shades of brown, red and black were lumped together. White, pale blue, pale green and yellow were frequently confused with each other. And all the while, grey skipped merrily across vibratory barriers and passed for everything.

Historical researchers have noted that man's earlier writings are almost completely devoid of color descriptions, which would seem to indicate a certain lack of sensitivity in this area. And it may be that an ancient Greek man gazed up at a bright blue sky, and let his eyes sweep over the jade and maroon horizon studded with mauve-tone Rosemary bushes. Unlike William Wordsworth, however, the Greek's heart did not "leap up" when he beheld a rainbow in the sky. Color awareness became a sophisticated development only in mankind's most recent history.

The color vibrations always existed somewhere, but man did not have the intellectual capacity to distinguish between the colors. Youngsters of today can handle color perception with more aplomb than most educated early royalty could have maintained. However, in earlier moments, as is still true today, an occasional "freak" was born. He may have been frightened by unusual "sensations" his modern eyes detected. And he probably remained silent most of the time rather than admit to such an undesirable abnormality. But if one waits long enough, the rest of the world catches up.

Pumpkin yellow, passionate pink, azure blue and psychedelic green have now left the poets, the dreamers and the schizoids and have turned on the bourgeoisie. Cavemen angels from way back in B.C., who had experienced extra sensory perception, now sigh in relief at their own vindication, and straighten their persimmon-tinted halos!

It has only been in the last hundred years or so that the aware and hungry eye was given the chemical conditions needed to transform fantasy into reality. The Dutch masters, with their monochromatic paintings, may not have been suffering from a lack of intellectual understanding, but rather, from a lack of the chemically produced "Prussian Blue." Gainsborough's "Blue Boy" was not only a charming portrait, but also a unique color experiment that was the most successful of its kind at the time. As the vague longings of man took on a definite form, he was able to create the proper environment needed to perpetuate his particular "freakishness," and comprehension accelerated. The ordinary lipstick counter of today is an example of how many ways man has devised to understand, to see, and then to categorize . . . PINK!

Sensational evolution rapidly expanded! All about us, more and more people are born who claim to see sights normal eyes never see, hear sounds normal ears never hear, know truths normal hearts never know. They are the 20th-Century Freaks, the cavemen of the Aquarian Age. They are the new pioneers.

While it may be lonely out there in the lush wilderness, one thing is certain: The colors are vivid in the sparkling clean air, and there's got to be an unbeatable excitement attached to stalking dinosaurs.

They used to laugh at people who spoke of ghosts in their houses, but today many universities have a department to investigate reports of the supernatural, extra sensory perception and other strange happenings that long have been spoken of but never satisfactorily explained. Those who scoffed at the idea that man might fly were replaced by descendants who were certain man would never travel to outer space. And now, what's beyond that?

Witches employ a strange power that they think they have explained to themselves. They know witchcraft works, but how much untapped power there is in the human mind, and where it comes from, may be things beyond explanation in terms of mere supernormal energy forces. The mysteries of the mind are as vast and unknown as the farthest star in the darkest skies. And it is only recently that man has learned to fly.